P9-ARO-957

Winter Saints

Stories for the Days of Advent and Christmas

Melissa Musick Nussbaum, storyteller

Judy Jarrett, artist

THIS BOOK BELONGS TO
BEEBE LIBRARY
345 MAIN STREET
WAKEFIELD, MA 01880

AND WAS FIRST READ IN THE YEAR

To my mother, Betty Curry Musick, who was always willing to make yet another trip to the library, the bookstore and the used magazine store. I am forever grateful.

Melissa Musick Nussbaum

I dedicate this book to Bill's memory.

Judy Jarrett

AKNOWLEDGMENTS

The saints of this and every season belong to us all. Many people tell their stories and keep their days. The author is indebted to these tellers of saint stories:

Taylor Branch, *Parting the Waters* (Simon and Schuster)

Butler's Lives of the Saints (Christian Classics)

David Cartlidge, David Dugan, eds., *Blessed Mary and the Childhood of Our Savior: Documents for the Study of the Gospels* (Fortress Press)

Ronda De Sola Chervin, *Treasury of Women Saints* (Servant Publications)

Robert Ellsberg, *All Saints* (The Crossroad Publishing Company)

Louis Ginzberg, *The Legends of the Jews* (The Jewish Publication Society of America)

Peter Mazar, *Winter* (Liturgy Training Publications)

Nathan Mitchell, "The RCIA at Twenty-Five: Retrospective and Prognosis," November 6 – 9, 1997 (North American Forum on the Catechumenate)

Charles R. Morris, *American Catholic* (Times Books)

Thomas O'Gorman, *An Advent Sourcebook* (Liturgy Training Publications)

Mary O'Neill, *Saints: Adventures in Courage* (Doubleday & Company)

Mary Ann Simcoe, *A Christmas Sourcebook* (Liturgy Training Publications)

Tasha Tudor, *Take Joy!* (Philomel Books)

Jacobus de Voragine, *The Golden Legend: Readings on the Saints* (Princeton University Press)

Excerpts from the English translation of Psalms 85, 96, 98 and 146 and of the Canticles of Zechariah and Mary from the *Liturgical Psalter*, © 1994, International Committee on English in the Liturgy, Inc. (ICEL). All rights reserved. Excerpt from *Letters and Papers from Prison* by Dietrich Bonhoeffer © SCM Press, The Enlarged Edition, 1971, p. 166. *Conditor Alme Siderum:* tune © 1986, G.I.A. Publications, Inc., all rights reserved; text, stanzas 1 and 3 © 1985 by Church Publishing, Inc.

Gabe Huck was the editor of this book with great assistance from Peter Mazar. Bryan Cones and Audrey Novak Riley were the production editors. Anna Manhart designed the book and Jim Mellody-Pizzato was the production artist who set the type in Veljovic, Motion and Frutiger. Printed in the United States of America.

Copyright © 1998, Archdiocese of Chicago: Liturgy Training Publications, 1800 North Hermitage Avenue, Chicago IL 60622-1101; 1-800-933-1800, fax 1-800-933-7094, e-mail orders@ltp.org. All rights reserved.

Library of Congress Catalog Card Number: 98-42842

ISBN 1-56854-246-1

WINST

03 02 01 00 99 98   10 9 8 7 6 5 4 3 2 1

LITURGY
TRAINING
PUBLICATIONS

Here are the stories of the Winter
Saints. All the days from late November
to early January have their saints
and each saint has a story.

When did the Winter Saints live?
And where did they live?

Turn this page to find a line of time.
Every Winter Saint is here, from Adam
and Eve to Maura Clarke and her
companions. And when you find a saint,
you'll find where to go in the book
for the saint's story.
Where are you on this line of time?

Then turn the page again and you'll
find a map. And on the maps you'll find
where Nicholas lived and where Lucy
lived and where Dorothy Day lived.
And where do you live?

As you read the stories, come back
to the line of time and to the map
and find each saint.

Now rejoice in the communion
of the saints!

When Did the Winter Saints Live?

Sarah
December 15

1500

Lucy
December 13

Hagar
December 14

Years before Jesus Was Born

John the Apostle
December 27

Adam and Eve
December 24

Years after Jesus Was Born

Thomas the Apostle
December 21

Andrew the Apostle
November 30

Lazarus
December 17

A Woman of Zorah
December 16

John the Baptizer
December 10

Hannah
December 18

Stephen
December 26

1000

Anna and Simeon
January 3

The Holy Family's
Flight into Egypt
January 1

Holy Innocents
December 28

Elijah's Chariot
December 9

Epiphany
January 6

0 Birth of the Lord
December 25

Annunciations to
Mary and Joseph
December 20

Anna and Joachim
December 8

Isaiah's Peace
November 27

Zechariah
and Elizabeth
December 19

500 Years before Jesus Was Born

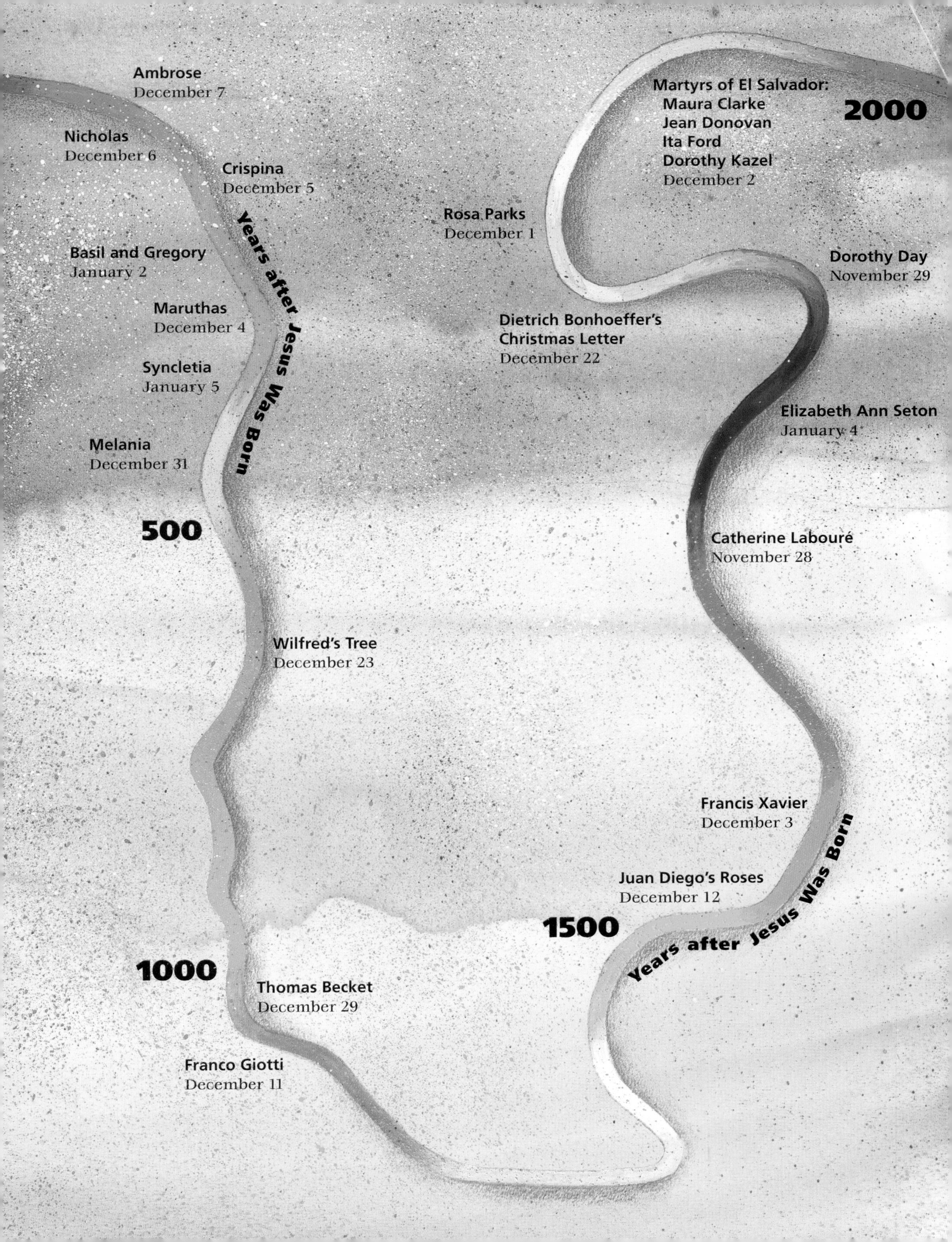

Ambrose
December 7

Nicholas
December 6

Crispina
December 5

Basil and Gregory
January 2

Maruthas
December 4

Syncletia
January 5

Melania
December 31

Years after Jesus Was Born

500

Wilfred's Tree
December 23

1000

Thomas Becket
December 29

Franco Giotti
December 11

Martyrs of El Salvador:
Maura Clarke
Jean Donovan
Ita Ford
Dorothy Kazel
December 2

2000

Rosa Parks
December 1

Dorothy Day
November 29

Dietrich Bonhoeffer's
Christmas Letter
December 22

Elizabeth Ann Seton
January 4

Catherine Labouré
November 28

Francis Xavier
December 3

Juan Diego's Roses
December 12

1500

Years after Jesus Was Born

Where Did the Winter Saints Live?

NORTH AMERICA

Dorothy Day
Elizabeth Ann Seton

Rosa Parks

Atlantic Ocean

Pacific Ocean

Juan Diego

Maura Clarke
Jean Donovan
Ita Ford
Dorothy Kazel

SOUTH AMERICA

EUROPE

North Sea

Wilfred

Thomas Becket

Dietrich Bonhoeffer

Catherine Labouré

Ambrose
Franco Giotti

Melania

Mediterranean Sea

Lucy

Andrew

Creator of the Stars of Night

Once, some summers ago, we were staying in a cabin high in the Colorado mountains. It was a long walk from our cabin to the bathhouse, and most nights we made the walk by the light of the stars.

That walk reminded me of times when I was very small, sitting on a bare mattress just before my mother put on fresh sheets. She would shake out the bottom sheet, letting it float over my head. It would be warm from the clothesline, still carrying the smell of the wind and the grass. I would close my eyes and feel the sheet settle along the curves and into the hollows of my body.

That's how, so it seems to me, stars look on a clear summer night in the mountains — as though God took a sheet of them, fresh off the line, and shook them out over our waiting heads. And I imagine as I close my eyes that the stars can settle along the curves and into the hollows of my body.

But on this night, while we took our showers and brushed our teeth in the bathhouse, clouds moved in and covered the stars. My daughter and I walked out into a darkness so deep that we stopped, suddenly unsure of that familiar walk. Anna clutched my hand and we began to move, slowly, testing the dirt with our toes before committing our feet flat and entire.

We could not talk. Finding our way took too much energy to leave any to spare. We stumbled on rocks and hesitated before imagined accidents. Our legs felt floppy and uncertain.

**Creator of the stars of night,
Your people's everlasting light,
O Christ, redeemer of us all,
We pray you hear us when we call.**

This is the first verse of an ancient and beautiful Advent hymn. It invites us to imagine the darkness before God sent light upon the earth. Imagine the night without the stars, without the moon.

Suddenly the Creator of the stars of night speaks the universe into being, and the light is so vivid, so sharp, so unexpected! This is the first light, light when we had never before known its kind.

Jesus, the Word who spoke the universe into being, comes into the universe as a human child. The world, so old and worn, is made new.

**Come, Sun and Savior, to embrace
Our gloomy world, its weary race,
As groom to bride, as bride to groom:
The wedding chamber, Mary's womb.**

Many of the people who have lived on our "gloomy world" would be surprised to hear that we call them saints. But they are the saints. The love of God shines brightly in their lives. It is their stories we will read in this book. They are the shining stars in the winter sky.

We'll enjoy quite a company: Catherine Labouré tending chickens, Crispina standing before a judge, Bishop Nicholas saving condemned prisoners, Elizabeth Ann Seton jumping rope with her children, Sarah and Hannah and Elizabeth waiting for their babies to be born, Thomas Becket opening a door to his killers, Melania freeing her slaves, Juan Diego with his arms full of flowers.

In all times and in all places, including our own, people have been drawn to their saints. We follow them as the Magi followed the star. And we find, as did the Magi, that they lead not to themselves or to their own brightness, but to the Creator of the light, the Creator of the stars of night.

Study War No More

This story is about a man named Isaiah. His name rhymes with "by the way, uh." When he was born, some 800 years before the birth of Jesus, the land of Israel had been split into two separate countries. The kingdom called Israel was in the north, which is why it is sometimes called the Northern Kingdom. The kingdom called Judah was in the south and so it is called the Southern Kingdom. Isaiah lived in Judah.

Even before Israel was divided, it was not a rich or powerful nation. Israel was like a hallway in the house of the Middle East. It was useful as a passageway, but not for much else. Surrounded by bigger, richer nations, Israel was often invaded by armies on their way from one country to another.

Still, no matter how bad it had been for Israel the undivided, it was worse for the two smaller kingdoms, which each now had yet another border to guard!

In time, the Northern Kingdom fell to a nation called Assyria, their neighbor to the northeast. The people in the south were afraid. Would they be the next to fall?

So the Southern Kingdom, Judah, began to make treaties, first with one neighbor and then another. The king of Judah hoped that powerful friends would protect Judah from harm. If Judah couldn't have a large army, if Judah couldn't make many weapons, then Judah's friends could. Judah even made a treaty with Assyria, the nation that had conquered Israel!

During these days, Isaiah was a priest in the temple in Jerusalem. God came to him asking, "Whom shall I send, and who will go for us?"

Egypt Isaiah answered God, saying, "Here I am! Send me."

So God sent Isaiah out into the kingdom of Judah. **God wanted Isaiah to warn the people not to trust in armies, not to trust in weapons, but to trust in God alone.**

Isaiah understood that a powerful army looks strong, just as a frozen pond looks solid. But can the ice hold a person's weight, or will the ice break up and send the stranded person into the icy waters? No one knows until the surface has been tested.

Isaiah begged the people of Judah to remember all that God had done. God had been tested and had been found faithful. Who brought the people of Israel into the land? Who gave them the wise and good king, David? God was strong. God could be trusted to hold them fast. God had held them fast for generations.

Isaiah called on the people of Judah to put down the weapons of war and to take up the weapons of God, which are mercy and justice, charity and truth. He said, "Cease to do evil, learn to do good; seek justice, correct oppression; defend the orphan, plead for the widow."

Assyria →

Israel

Judah

• Jerusalem

Isaiah was not happy with the job God had given him to do, for no one wanted to hear what Isaiah was saying. Make solid steel swords into plows? Turn soldiers into farmers to raise food for hungry orphans? How would that protect Judah?

Isaiah knew that no one believed him. He saw that Judah would continue on its destructive path. But Isaiah also knew how strong God's love is for all creation. After a time of suffering, Isaiah said, another day will dawn, and people will rejoice. Isaiah said:

**"The people who walked in darkness
have seen a great light;
Those who dwell in a land of deep darkness,
on them has light shined.
You have brought them abundant joy
and great rejoicing.
For the yoke that burdened them,
the pole on their shoulder,
And the rod of their taskmaster
you have smashed."**

Catherine Labouré, A Surprising Saint

Some saints lived exciting and busy lives. Every day must have been filled with thrilling adventures. But some saints lived dull lives. They didn't do much out of the ordinary. Still, even dull people can surprise us.

A surprising saint was named Catherine Labouré. She was born in France in the year 1806. Catherine had many brothers and sisters. Of all of them, she was the only one who never learned to read or write. Perhaps that's because Catherine had no time to study. Her mother died when Catherine was only eight years old, and she began taking care of the house and her large family.

In those days, no one had washing machines or microwave ovens. Catherine had to haul water from a well for her family to drink and to wash and to cook. She had to build a fire in a wood-burning stove to bake. It was a hard life.

When Catherine was 14 she told her father she wanted to enter a religious community. She wanted to become a Sister of Charity of Saint Vincent de Paul.

Catherine was not a leader in her community of sisters. As she had done at home, Catherine did the hard jobs, the jobs that must be done again and again, the jobs many of us don't like to do. But she did her work with care and found goodness there. Catherine looked after the chickens, feeding them and watering them. She cleaned their pens and gathered their eggs, still warm from the hens' bodies. Catherine treated the chickens when they fell ill. She probably named each hen and rooster, for she came to know them well. Catherine did this work day after day.

There is never a holiday from raising chickens.

One of the leaders in her community later described Catherine as "rather dull." But Catherine, the surprising saint, had a surprising prayer life. It was anything but dull! Three different times Jesus' mother, the Virgin Mary, appeared to Catherine.

The first time, Catherine saw "a shining child" who led her into the chapel. There she saw Mary and talked with her for two full hours. Mary told Catherine that difficult times were ahead for her and for the church.

Twice more Mary came to Catherine. They talked together like friends. They talked together like mother and daughter. For a woman who had lost her mother when she was still a young girl, these must have been good talks and good times.

One might think Catherine would wake the whole community with her news. It isn't every day a person has a heart-to-heart talk with someone from heaven, and Catherine did this three times! But Catherine told no one of the visits Mary made to her, and of their hours together. Perhaps she thought no one would believe a chicken farmer, a woman who could neither read nor write. Or perhaps she did not wish to become a curiosity, no longer simply Catherine, but "that weird woman who sees visions." Perhaps she did not have the words to tell what she had seen and heard and felt when she was with Mary. It would be hard to explain a hug to someone who has never been touched, or the feel of summer mud between toes to someone who has always worn shoes.

Whatever the reason, Catherine just kept living her "rather insignificant" life. She began working in the community hospice, caring for the aged and the dying. She continued to care for her flock of chickens.

Then, shortly before she died, Catherine told the leader of her community of the times Mary had come and of how she had made herself known.

When Catherine died, the word of her surprising life spread. Catherine may not have been the one most people would choose to receive a vision of Mary, but she was the one God chose. And this is the day the church remembers her.

Dorothy Day Dances

Dorothy Day was a woman who loved abundance. She liked the smell of roasting meat and baking bread and steaming vegetables and onions frying in a pan. She liked the sound of opera, the soaring notes of sopranos who dressed in billowing skirts and shining jewels, and who sang of lost love. She liked the look of large, sunny rooms filled with flowers and books and comfortable chairs. She liked the feel of fine fabrics, silks and wools and crisp, summer cottons against her skin. She liked to sit up all night long, eating and drinking and talking with friends. But she loved nothing and no one as she loved Christ.

Dorothy didn't just respect Christ, or think Christ an interesting person from a long-ago time, or show an interest in Christ only at Christmas and Easter. Dorothy was in love with Christ, and she wanted what all lovers want — to be with the beloved.

So Dorothy searched her heart and the scriptures and the stories of the holy men and women, the stories handed down from one generation to the next. Where did Jesus spend his time? Where were saints to be found? They spent their days with the ones most in need of God's mercy — with the despised and the rejected, the outcast and the poor. And that's where Dorothy would spend her days, too.

In 1933, Dorothy Day, the woman who loved beauty, opened a "house of hospitality" called Maryhouse for the poor of New York City. The weary, the unwashed, the ill, the desperate, the hungry, the lonely, the fearful — they found their way to Dorothy's door.

Through the years, Dorothy helped staff many houses of hospitality. The work was never easy. The houses were in neighborhoods of broken windows and garbage-strewn streets and noisy fights. Dorothy wrote of one morning when

"to ward off the noise I have my radio on. As Saint Teresa said as she grabbed her castanets and started to dance in her unheated convent, 'One must do something to make life bearable!'"

It wasn't that Dorothy ever came to prefer poverty to comfort, or hard work to relaxation, or fasting to feasting. She wrote, "All families should have the conveniences and comforts which modern living brings and which do simplify life, and give time to read, to study, to think, and to pray. . . . But poverty is my vocation."

Christ had led Dorothy to poverty, and she never stopped following Christ. Dorothy would go wherever Christ led. In whatever lowly form Christ took, Dorothy would serve him, feed him, house him, bind his wounds.

On November 29, 1980, just as the season of Advent was beginning, Dorothy died. William Miller tells a wonderful story about her funeral, a funeral where the lifted-up and the bowed-down came together.

"At the church door, Cardinal Terence Cooke met the body to bless it. As the procession stopped for this rite, a demented person pushed his way through the crowd and, bending low over the coffin, peered at it intently. No one interfered, because, as even the funeral directors understood, it was in such as this man that Dorothy had seen the face of God."

Andrew: X Marks the Spot

Andrew and his brother Simon were fishermen. They didn't fish with poles and hooks and bait. They used a big net, called a casting net, which they lowered into the Sea of Galilee.

One day Jesus was walking along the seashore and he stopped to watch Andrew and Simon at work. He saw that they were skilled with a net, and called out to them, "Andrew! Simon! Come with me.

I will make you fish for men and women."

Were the brothers surprised to hear this stranger telling them to quit working and follow him? Did the brothers laugh to imagine their nets filled with freshly caught people?

Andrew and Simon (later Jesus gave him the name Peter) put down their nets and followed Jesus. They did not say goodbye to their families. They didn't sell their business. They didn't even pack their clothes! They just left the boat and the nets and went wherever Jesus went. They became the first disciples of Jesus. For Andrew it was the beginning of a great adventure.

Andrew never stopped telling people about Jesus. Many stories are told about the journeys he made after Jesus died and rose from the dead. Some say he went to Turkey to preach the good news of Jesus. Some say he went to Scotland. Some say he went to Greece. Those who tell about Andrew in Greece say that the wife of the governor of the city of Patras got to know him. She listened to all that Andrew told her about Jesus. She came to believe that Jesus is the Savior of the world.

This made her husband, the governor, angry. He had Andrew arrested and brought before him. The governor demanded that Andrew worship the gods of Patras. But Andrew had walked with Jesus for a long time. He would not betray him now.

The governor decided to crucify Andrew, just as Jesus was crucified. Andrew thanked the governor because he wanted to follow Jesus in all things, in life and in death. Andrew's thankfulness made the governor even angrier. To spite Andrew, he ordered that the cross be built not in the shape of the letter "T," like Jesus' cross, but in the shape of an "X."

Most people know this "X" cross by the name of the one who hung upon it, faithful to the end. We call it "Saint Andrew's cross."

Rosa Parks **W**ill Not Be Moved

December 1

Stories are told about mighty warriors who conquer nations with guns and tanks, but some warriors carry no weapons. Some warriors are armed only with a dream and the will to make the dream come true.

An African American child, Rosa Parks, was born in Tuskegee, Alabama, in 1913, just fifty years after the end of slavery in the United States. Though slavery had been abolished, life was still hard for African Americans. The idea that black men and women were born to serve their white neighbors had deep roots in some people's minds. This idea was so strong that laws were enacted to keep blacks and whites apart. Whites rode in the front of the bus, blacks in the back. Whites used one public drinking fountain or restroom, and blacks used another. This system was called "segregation," and these laws were called "separate but equal" laws, but the restrooms and the drinking fountains were never equal.

Maybe white children weren't told just why they couldn't drink from the "Colored Only" fountain. Maybe black children weren't told just why they couldn't use the "Whites

feel good and not curl all the days

Only" restroom at the local department store. But children must have learned very early that to do such things would make serious trouble. To cross that line would be to declare war on a way of life, a way of life that ordered people by skin color: whites on the top, blacks on the bottom.

Rosa grew up. Her parents hoped their only child would finish high school. They thought she might even go on to college. But Rosa's mother fell ill, and Rosa dropped out of school to care for her. Still, she never stopped learning. She studied the works of Mohandas Gandhi and became a student of nonviolent protest and of peaceful change. And she became ever more convinced that life for blacks in the United States had to change — not someday, but in her lifetime.

Rosa became a tailor's assistant in Montgomery, Alabama. Every day she rode the bus to work and every day she rode the bus home again. So did most of the black workers in Montgomery. What Rosa saw made her angry! The buses of Montgomery were divided into three sections: the rear for blacks, the front for whites and a middle row of seats called "no man's land." If the back of the bus was full and if no whites needed the seats in the middle, blacks were allowed to ride in "no man's land." But if white riders boarded the bus and found the white section full, then the driver would say to black passengers in the middle, "Give me those seats." Even though blacks and whites paid the same fare, and even though a black passenger had claimed the seat first, if a white person wanted the seat, blacks had to move.

Rosa and her friends spent hours before and after church services planning a way to make the bus system of Montgomery treat all its riders fairly. They knew that more blacks than whites rode buses. They knew that if the blacks of the community all agreed to stop riding a bus line, to boycott a bus line, it would hurt the company and call attention to demands for fair treatment. But what event would bring the black community together in such an action? Brave Rosa agreed to be the one to strike the spark.

On December 1, 1955, a weary Rosa Parks left work and boarded the bus for home. She had given birth to a daughter just two weeks before. She had worked a full day. She needed to sit down. She took a seat in the "no man's land" section. The bus was full, and the driver noticed a white man standing beside him. He told all the black passengers in the middle seats to get up. Rosa politely refused. She said, "I'm not in the white section. I'm in no man's land."

The driver answered, "The white section is wherever I say it is." Then he threatened to arrest her.

Rosa must have been afraid, but she knew her cause was just. She said,

"Do what you have to do. I am not moving."

Rosa Parks was arrested. Her arrest set off a bus boycott in Montgomery that lasted 381 days. It was the beginning of the end of legal segregation in the United States.

roll down like mighty waters. Let right for justice flow like an ever-running stream

Four Martyrs of El Salvador

Dorothy

Some saints lived a long time ago. They lived before anyone had even dreamed of planes or telephones, radios or computers. But some saints live in our own time. They shop in malls and go to movies and drive on freeways. There, in towns and homes like our own, four young American women grew up.

Their names are **Maura Clarke, Jean Donovan, Ita Ford** and **Dorothy Kazel.** Maura and Ita were Maryknoll sisters. Dorothy was an Ursuline sister. Jean was a laywoman. They heard the gospel proclaimed, the words of Jesus, who said, "I was hungry and you gave me food, I was thirsty and you gave me drink, a stranger and you welcomed me, naked and you clothed me, ill and you cared for me, in prison and you visited me, for whatever you did for one of the least of mine, you did for me."

They heard those words, and they heard the call of Christ. And each woman set out to answer the call—to feed the hungry, to welcome the stranger, to clothe the naked, to care for the sick, to visit those in prison. It was a call that brought them, by different paths, to the small country of El Salvador.

In the 1970s a war was raging in El Salvador. Children were left orphaned.

Jean

Women were left widowed. Farmers could not plow or plant or harvest in fields laced with mines or ruined by the trampling boots of soldiers. Villages were burned and the villagers left homeless. Maura Clarke wrote to a friend, "We are trying to help the refugees—bringing them to shelters and getting food to places where it is desperately needed."

The people of El Salvador lived in fear, and so did the four women who had come to help. Maura and Ita and Dorothy and Jean thought about leaving, about returning to the safety of their homes and communities in the United States. Jean wrote to a friend, "Several times

I have decided to leave — I almost could except for the children, the poor bruised victims of adult lunacy. Who would care for them? Whose heart could be so staunch as to favor the reasonable thing in a sea of tears and loneliness? Not mine, dear friend, not mine."

So the women stayed on, sheltering refugees, delivering supplies to the needy, encouraging the weary and speaking always, with their words and their deeds, for peace.

It is a curious thing: The four women had no guns or troops at their command. They were not wealthy or well-known. Still, the soldiers of El Salvador feared them. They feared the power of their strong love of God. They feared the power of their strong love for the poor.

On December 2, 1980, Maura and Ita were flying back to El Salvador after a meeting. Dorothy and Jean drove to the airport to pick them up. Soldiers followed their car. The soldiers watched and followed as the four women met and embraced and began the journey home. Somewhere on a dark and quiet Salvadoran highway, the women were stopped and ordered from their car. The soldiers shot each woman. Then they buried their bodies in a cow pasture.

Maura Clarke had written to a friend of her fear. She had seen so much suffering, and she wondered how she would face her own suffering. She wrote, "One cries out, 'Lord, how long?' And then too what creeps into my mind is the little fear or big, that when it touches me very personally, will I be faithful?"

Maura and Ita and Dorothy and Jean were faithful. In life and in death, they were faithful. Only death could stop them from doing the good Jesus asks us all to do.

Francis Xavier Journeys Far from Home

When Francis Xavier left his parents' home in Spain and went north to the city of Paris, France, to study, he had no idea of the adventures that lay before him. He probably planned to return to Spain and to live there, near his family. He probably planned to marry and have children. But at the University of Paris, Francis met another fellow from Spain, a man named Ignatius. That man, Ignatius of Loyola, would change Francis' life.

Ignatius and Francis and six other friends came together to form a religious community they called the Society of Jesus. They believed God wanted them to go all over the world, even to the unfamiliar parts of the world, to tell people about Jesus. They didn't go as tourists. They went to stay, and many, like Francis, never returned to their homes again. They lived and died as one of the people they served.

These men lived in exciting times. European explorers were just beginning to travel all over the world. They were sailing to the Americas, to Africa, to Asia. In the year 1541, when Francis was 35, he sailed to India.

The voyage took over a year, and Francis arrived in a region called Goa. He was weary from traveling and discouraged by what he found. There were Indian

Christians in Goa, but the European Christians who had recently moved there were unkind to their Indian brothers and sisters.

The Europeans couldn't be bothered to learn the local languages, and they taught that dark-skinned people were less in the eyes of God than light-skinned people. How could anyone hear of the love of God from people who didn't love them? Francis wrote that what he saw there "left a permanent bruise on my soul."

So Francis got to work. He wanted the men and women of every country to hear the good news of Jesus. Francis must have wondered, "How can I be a good messenger?" First, Francis learned the language of the people.

He put away the clothes he had brought over on the boat and began to dress as the people around him dressed.

He ate what the people ate. If the poor slept on the floor, then Francis slept on the floor!

In this way, Francis traveled all along the southern coast of India. The word spread that this man lived what he taught. The word spread among many of the people of India that Francis knew a God who cherished the lowly and raised them high.

Five years after Francis arrived in India he began traveling to other parts of Asia. He sailed to Japan and stayed there for about two years. Then Francis left Japan and tried to sail to China. But he never set foot on the Chinese mainland. Francis had grown weary and ill over the long voyages, and he died on December 3, 1552.

We honor Francis as the patron saint of all those men and women — they might be Nigerians in New York or Canadians in Costa Rica — who do the work of Christ far from their homes and families.

ig Maruthas

Some artists draw pictures of saints and make all the women beautiful and all the men handsome. Their hair is clean and nicely combed, their teeth are even and shiny, and every saint stands slender and straight, gazing day and night at the heavens. If the saints ever move at all, they seem to glide along, as though they had wheels instead of feet.

But saints are people, and, like all people, saints come in different shapes and sizes, each with his or her own face and hair and body. Some are graceful and some are clumsy. Today we remember a clumsy and unwieldy saint, one who is very much loved in the nation of Syria but little known in our part of the world. This saint was a bishop, a man named Maruthas.

Maruthas lived nearly 1600 years ago in a town near the border of Persia, the country we now call Iran. When Maruthas was the bishop of his community, the ruler of

Syria was a man named Sapor, and he was no friend of the Christians. Sapor ordered the Christians of Syria arrested and imprisoned and sometimes killed. Maruthas collected the stories of the faithful men and women, called martyrs, who died in these persecutions. He told their stories and recorded them for later generations to read and hear. He wrote hymns in praise of the martyrs. Many of these hymns are still sung in the Christian churches of Syria.

But Maruthas hoped to do more. He hoped to stop the arrests and the killings. He wanted to have no more new stories to tell about the martyrs! So he went to the emperor in Constantinople, a city in the country we now call Turkey, and he pleaded with the emperor to come to the aid of the persecuted church in Syria. The emperor in Constantinople had power over the ruler of Syria, so Maruthas knew he could help.

Maruthas was not the only bishop staying in Constantinople. He found many others there, all asking the emperor for help with one problem or another. There were so many bishops in the court of the emperor that there wasn't much room to walk around.

And, since Maruthas was very fat and not very nimble, he had a hard time getting through the crowds.

One day, Maruthas was edging through the throngs of people when he stepped on the foot of Bishop Cyrinus of Chalcedon. He landed with his full weight on poor Cyrinus, whose skin was torn open. Cyrinus's foot became badly infected, and, since this was long before anyone had thought of antibiotics, Cyrinus died of the infection.

This must have made Maruthas, who was a gentle man, very upset and very sad — especially since Maruthas was known far and wide as a healer. Once, at the Persian court, Maruthas found the king confined to bed with terrible headaches. Every doctor in the land had seen the king, but none could help him.

Now the king, whose name was Yezdigerd, was not a Christian, and he was suspicious of this foreign bishop. But the king's pain was so severe that he allowed Maruthas to try to bring about a cure. So Maruthas consulted the medical books, and he prayed, and he cured the king's headaches.

The grateful king called the Syrian bishop "the friend of God" and decreed that the Christians of Persia be allowed to live and worship in freedom and in peace. For a while, at least, there would be no new martyrs.

In Syria, where Maruthas has the honor of being called a Doctor of the Church, he is remembered as a man so kind and wise that even his enemies honored him. So poor Bishop Cyrinus, who was never Maruthas's enemy, must have forgiven him too, this holy and clumsy saint.

Crispina and the Judge

Almost 1700 years ago, a woman named Crispina lived in north Africa. She was a wife and a mother and a faithful follower of Christ.

In those days, north Africa was ruled by the Roman Empire. The emperor was a man named Diocletian, and he feared and despised the followers of Christ. Diocletian believed that Christian worship was angering the gods of Rome and causing the gods to bring harm to the Romans. He ordered that Christians all over the empire be arrested and brought before the local authorities. He said, "If they will deny Christ, they may live. If they will not deny Christ, they must die."

We do not know where Crispina was when she was arrested. Maybe she was at home, cooking dinner for her family. Maybe she and her children were taking a pot of soup to a sick neighbor. Maybe she was telling stories of Jesus to the men and women of her town. Maybe she and her husband were just out walking.

We do know what happened after she was arrested because the judge, whose name was Anulinus, kept a record of the questions he asked her and the answers she gave.

Crispina must have been very afraid. Who would take care of her children while she was in jail? Who would take care of her children if she died? But she was very brave and very strong. Sometimes she was even funny.

Anulinus asked, "Don't you know the law? The law says you must worship the gods of the emperor."

Crispina answered, "I will only worship the one true God and our Lord, Jesus Christ, God's Son, who was born and suffered for us."

Anulinus said, "You are stubborn and disrespectful and vain, and you will be punished."

Crispina did not mean to be stubborn or disrespectful or vain. She just wanted to go home. She did not want to be punished. But she would not, could not, lie. "If it is necessary," she said, "I will suffer for my faith."

The judge must have thought Crispina didn't fully understand what he was saying. So he told her, "You will lose your head if you do not obey the emperor. All Africa obeys the emperor, and so must you."

Crispina answered him, "The emperor's religion is not a true faith. No true religion forces unwilling people to believe."

Of course, Crispina was right, and Anulinus knew she was right, but he didn't want to argue with her any more. He wanted this stubborn woman to obey the law so that they could all go home. He said, "You don't have to believe. Just go to the emperor's temple and bow your head and copy what the others are doing there. This is the way to look after your own safety."

Crispina said, "I do not fear what you threaten, but I do fear turning from God.

Would you have me turn against the one who gives me life?"

Anulinus persisted, "Crispina, I am telling you the law of the emperor. It cannot be wrong to obey his law."

Crispina was surprised. "God made the sea and the green plants and the dry land. What has the emperor made, that I should put him before God?"

The judge decided to frighten Crispina into obedience. He had her head shaved, and then he brought her before a jeering mob. He threatened, "If you do not worship the gods of Rome, I will have you beheaded."

And Crispina, whose heart was still merry, said, "Well, thank God, being beheaded isn't as bad as worshiping idols. I should certainly lose my head if I start worshiping them!"

The judge, who did not think Crispina was a bit funny, looked around at the mob and said, "Can we endure this impious Crispina any longer?"

So Crispina was killed with a sword. As she lay dying, she cried out, "Praise to God who delivered me out of your hands." It was December 5th, in the year 304.

icholas the Wonder-worker

Bishops are called to teach, to lead and to reveal the holiness of all God has made. It's possible that no one was ever as good at "bishoping" as Nicholas. It is said that he was born long ago in a place called Patera, along the coast in a country we now call Turkey.

Nicholas was the only child of wealthy parents, and he had every toy and comfort a child could wish. But when Nicholas's parents died and he inherited their riches, he never thought of the money as his. Nicholas believed everything on the earth and in the heavens is God's property.

Early in his life, Nicholas used the riches to help those in need. Many stories are told about his care for the destitute and distressed. Perhaps the most famous story is the one about a poor man and his daughters. The man was so poor that he could not feed his family. He decided to sell his daughters into slavery. When Nicholas heard of the desperate and wicked plan, he crept to the man's house in the middle of the night and threw three bags of gold into an open window. The daughters were saved!

Nicholas often did his good work in secret, but sometimes a bishop has to lead out in the open, in the light of day. Once Nicholas found out that three men had been condemned to death. So he dressed up in his bishop's robes and went to the site of the execution. He was almost too late! As he arrived, the executioner was holding a sword high over the heads of the prisoners. The executioner was ready to chop off their heads! If Nicholas had more time, he might have

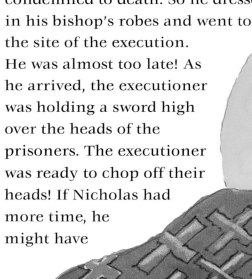

argued the case before a judge, but there wasn't a moment to spare. Nicholas grabbed the executioner's sword.

No matter how the man tugged and pulled, Nicholas would not let go.

Nicholas untied the prisoners. They trembled with surprise and relief, and he set them free.

Another story is told about a terrible famine. People were dying from hunger. Bishop Nicholas heard that ships loaded with grain were docked in the harbor. Again Nicholas put on his billowing robes, and he marched down to the dock. He begged the sailors to spare some grain for his hungry people.

"Father Nicholas," the sailors said, "we would like to help you. But this grain was carefully measured when we sailed from the granaries in Egypt, and it will be carefully measured again when we reach our destination. If any grain is missing, we will lose our lives as a punishment."

Nicholas trusted in God. He said, "Do not be afraid to do what is right. Share the grain, and I promise you, in God's power, that the inspectors will not find any missing."

The sailors trusted God, too, and gave a good portion of the grain to Nicholas. When they arrived at their destination, they still had the same amount of grain as when they left Egypt! The sailors began to praise God and to tell everyone about the wisdom and faith of Bishop Nicholas. And the people of Nicholas' town had enough grain to eat and enough grain left over to plant as seed for next year's harvest.

When holy bishop Nicholas died (probably in the year 341), the whole church gathered to bury him. It was December 6.

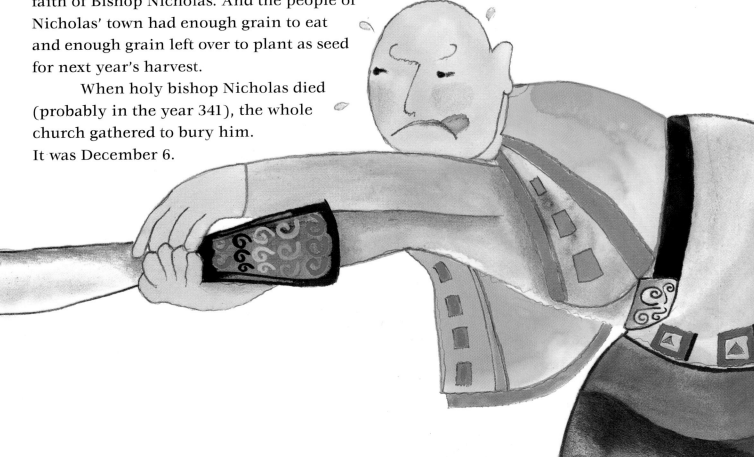

Ambrose the Poet Bishop

Ambrose began his life serving one master and ended it serving another. He was born about 1700 years ago, the son of an important Roman official. His father was the governor of the lands we now call England and Ireland and Spain and France. Ambrose grew up around powerful people, and he was never frightened by those in authority.

The Roman emperor named him the governor of northern Italy. Ambrose moved to the city of Milan to begin his job, and he immediately had something to say about everyone else. Ambrose never kept his thoughts to himself. People around him described him as feisty.

At the cathedral in Milan, the bishop's church, an argument broke out over who would be the next bishop. Some wanted one man, others another. Everyone was angry and no one would give in. Fights broke out.

Ambrose waded into the crowd. He called for people to calm down. What a surprise when the rioters stopped yelling at one another and began yelling for Ambrose to be named the new bishop of Milan!

In those days many Christians waited until late in life to be baptized. So, even though Ambrose believed in Jesus as the Christ, he was not yet baptized. He was certain that God and the people of the church had called him to be bishop, so he had a lot to do in a very short time. In just one week, he was baptized, confirmed and made his first communion in the celebration of eucharist. Next he received the holy orders of priest and bishop on December 7, 374! Then he started studying. Ambrose wanted to learn all that he could. He wanted to be worthy of the people who had called him to serve.

Ambrose was fierce in God's service. He didn't even fear the emperor, a man named Theodosius. When the emperor allowed his soldiers to kill innocent citizens, Ambrose demanded that Theodosius stand in front of the people and ask God and the people for forgiveness. But the emperor was afraid that this would make him look weak. Ambrose told Theodosius that the emperor is not above the church, but in the church. And the emperor did what Ambrose asked him to do.

Bishop Ambrose saw that the Roman governor was allowing false worship in one of the churches. So Ambrose called on the people to follow him into the church. They stayed there singing and singing. It must have been a scary time. At any minute the governor might send in the police to break up their protest.

The people sang songs that Ambrose himself had written. Neighboring bishops said they wished the Christians in their cities would sing as well as the Christians of Milan. Ambrose was a great songwriter, and we still sing some of his songs today. One is the beautiful Christmas hymn, "Redeemer of the Nations."

Redeemer of the nations,
Make known your wondrous birth
Which so befits your grandeur
And sanctifies the earth.
A virgin was your mother,
O holy mystery!
Let all creation marvel
At your nativity.

Birth of Mary: Grandma Anna and Grandpa Joachim

Many stories are told about the birth of Mary. Saint Jerome, who lived about 1600 years ago, wrote down the stories of Mary that he remembered hearing in his childhood. This is one of those stories.

There was a man named Joachim (whose name rhymes with "sew a seam") who married a woman named Anna. They lived in Israel and they served God all their days.

Anna and Joachim divided everything they owned into three equal parts: one part to give for the work of the temple, one part to give for the care of the poor, and one part to keep for their own needs. There was not much they wanted for themselves, but they did long for a child. Year after year they waited and prayed, but no child was born to them.

Once, when Joachim went to place his offering on the temple altar, he was turned away. In front of everyone the priest said, "Joachim, you know what the law says. A man who cannot father children, who has made no increase among the people of God, cannot stand here with those who can father children."

Joachim left the temple and went out into the fields. He was ashamed and did not want to face the friends and family members who had heard the priest turn him away.

When Joachim was alone, an angel came to him and said: "Do not be ashamed because you and Anna are childless. Was not Sarah the mother of the Hebrew people? And was she not childless for 90 years? Then, did she not bear Isaac, to whom was promised the blessing of all nations? Who was stronger than Samson or holier than Samuel? Yet their parents could not have children, either. God has heard your prayers.

Anna will bear a child, a daughter, and you are to name her Mary. She will be filled

with the Holy Spirit from her mother's womb. She will serve God all her days."

While Joachim was listening to the angel, poor Anna was home weeping in her garden. She watched a mother sparrow feeding her young and thought how happy the sparrow must be. Anna had no child, and now, it seemed, she had no husband! Where could he be? Had Joachim abandoned her because she could not bear a child?

Then the angel who appeared to Joachim came to Anna. The angel told her all that Joachim had heard, and more besides. The angel said, "Go to Jerusalem's Golden Gate. You will meet your husband there. He is coming home to you."

Anna ran from her garden, and Joachim ran from the field! They met at the Golden Gate, and there they kissed and embraced and praised God for the blessing that was promised them. Then Anna and Joachim went home together and waited for the day when their beloved daughter, Mary, would be born.

Swing Low, Sweet Chariot

Elijah worked throughout his life as God's prophet in Israel. He had followed God all his days, and now his days were coming to their end. God sent Elijah to find a man named Elisha, whose name means "God has saved." Elisha would take Elijah's place as prophet in Israel.

Elijah set out and came upon Elisha plowing his fields. Elisha was following twelve yoke of oxen as they worked the ground for planting. Elijah walked up to Elisha and threw his cloak over him. This meant that Elijah was handing on his power to be a prophet.

Elisha left his plow and his oxen and ran after Elijah. He cried, "Please, let me kiss my mother and father goodbye and I will follow you." But then Elisha realized something. There was no time to say goodbye to his parents. There was no time to finish plowing the fields. Elisha had to leave everything, just as it was, right at that moment, and follow Elijah.

The time soon came for God to take Elijah up to heaven. He and Elisha stood at the Jordan River. Elijah took his cloak, the one he had thrown over Elisha in the field, and rolled it up. He struck the river with the rolled-up cloak, and the water parted before them. Elijah and Elisha walked through the riverbed on dry ground!

After they crossed over, Elijah said to Elisha, "Ask what you want of me, before I am taken from you." Now, in those days, a father's first-born son received a double share of the children's inheritance. And that is what Elisha asked of Elijah, his father in faith. He said, "May I receive a double portion of your spirit?"

Elijah answered, "If you see me taken up from you, your request will be granted." And they walked on, talking.

Just then, a chariot pulled by horses came between them. This was not like any chariot Elijah and Elisha had ever seen. This chariot was flaming, and the horses were flaming. They were on fire, but they did not burn up! A whirlwind blew around the fiery chariot and swept Elijah up. As Elisha stood and watched, Elijah went up to heaven in the fiery whirlwind!

Elisha cried out, "My father!" He tore his own cloak in two and picked up the cloak Elijah had left behind.

Then Elisha rolled up the cloak as Elijah had done and struck the waters of the river and the Jordan divided, and Elisha walked through on dry ground. God had indeed rested Elijah's spirit on Elisha.

John the Baptizer

When Herod was king of Galilee, a man named John came out of the desert. His looks were rough and his manner was gruff. He wore the skin of a camel draped over his body. He ate honey that he stole from bees, and he ate grasshoppers.

John preached to the people, and even his words sounded wild. He called on men and women to be like trees that bear sweet and abundant fruit. Fruitless people were like barren trees that are only useful to be chopped up for firewood. John spoke angrily to people who said they loved God but who were cruel to one another. He called them a "nest of vipers."

Of course, most people didn't like being compared to a heap of snakes. They also didn't like hearing that they are good for nothing but kindling.

Still, some people knew that John was telling the truth, even if it was unpleasant. They followed him. They told others about him. But John said: **"Another is coming who is mightier than I. He is so mighty that I am not worthy to unfasten the straps of his sandals. I baptize you in water, but he will baptize you in the Holy Spirit."**

King Herod took his brother's wife, Herodias, to be his own wife. John told the king that this was wrong. Herod was angry, and Herodias was even angrier. She wanted John killed. But Herod was afraid to harm a holy man, so, instead, he had John arrested. Sometimes Herod would go to John's prison cell and talk to him. He was fascinated with John, even though the prophet's words troubled him.

Herod's birthday came, and he threw a big party for all the rich people of Galilee. Salome, Herodias' daughter, danced before the king and all his guests. Herod was so pleased with the girl's performance that he said, "Ask me for anything. I will give you half my kingdom if that's what you want."

Salome went to her mother and said, "What should I ask for?" Herodias remembered the man she hated. She told Salome, "Ask for the head of John the Baptist."

Salome ran back to the king. "I want the head of John the Baptist," she told Herod. "I want it brought to me on a platter."

Now Herod probably thought Salome would ask for jewels or gold or a fine house and many servants. He was astounded and afraid when he heard what she wanted. But he had given his word in front of his guests. If he refused the girl, his guests would laugh at him.

So Herod sent a soldier to kill John. The soldier returned with John's head. Herod had the head put on a platter and presented to Salome. She gave it to her mother.

John's friends came in sorrow. They took his body and placed it in a tomb.

Franco Takes a Hike

Some saints grow up longing to serve Jesus. But other saints spend years running from God. The very last thing they want to do is serve Jesus.

Franco Lippi was one of these reluctant saints. Anyone who knew Franco would have guessed him more likely to wind up on a wanted poster than in a book of stories about holy men and women!

Franco was born in the year 1211 in the town of Siena in the country we now call Italy. He was a lazy child, hateful to his parents and violent toward his friends. Franco's father tried to make his son behave, but soon the heartsick father died. Franco went on a binge—he spent all his money gambling and was even suspected of murdering a man. Franco did not want to stand trial for murder. Who would testify on his behalf?

So Franco ran away and joined a gang of thieves. With them he spent many years doing exactly as he pleased, giving no thought to whether something was right or wrong. He drank so much that he ruined his health. Twice Franco almost died. Then, when he was 50 years old, Franco went blind. He was scared and shocked, and he began, for the first time in his life, to long for God.

Franco began a pilgrimage to the shrine of the apostle James at Compostela, in Spain. **Imagine walking all the way from Italy to Spain without being able to see where you're going!**

The journey took Franco a very long time and allowed him to think deeply about many things. Finally he reached Compostela and knelt in prayer. His blindness was healed, his sight was restored!

Franco's physical sight returned, and, even more wonderfully, the spiritual sight he had developed in his blindness never left him. He walked barefoot all the way from Compostela to Rome. He was praying in a church in Rome when he had a vision of Mary. She told Franco that he must make amends for all the hurt and harm he had caused in Siena. So he left for home.

It's doubtful that many townspeople were glad to see Franco walking the streets of Siena once again. Wasn't he the no-good thief, the gambler and the drunk?

In Siena and in other cities there were groups of men who lived together as brothers. They were devoted to prayer. Some groups of brothers called themselves "Carmelites," after Mount Carmel in the Holy Land, a mountain where the prophet Elijah had once lived. When Franco asked the Carmelites in Siena if he could join them, they were, of course, suspicious. How could such a wicked person change? Was he trying to fool them? The Carmelites said, "Franco, we don't know if we can trust you or not. Come back in five years. Then we'll be able to tell if you are really a changed man." Since Franco was 65 years old, they probably thought that in five years he would be dead!

Franco did not become angry or violent, as once he would have done. He simply went back to his life of prayer and charity. Five years later, at the age of 70, he returned to the Carmelites and was received into their community as a brother.

Franco lived for ten years as a Carmelite. Not only his Carmelite brothers but the whole town of Siena came to know him as a gentle man of faith and truth. Franco was truly sorry for every hurtful thing he had done, and he spent the last years of his long life trying to undo his many wrongs.

Franco died on December 11, in the season of Advent, in the year 1291.

Siena •

Rome •

Roses in December

When Juan Diego was born over 400 years ago, his mother and father had never heard of Jesus. They were Aztec people, living in the country we now call Mexico, and they worshiped a god the Aztecs called the mother goddess.

Juan was not very old when the Spanish explorers came to his land. Soldiers came, then Catholic missionaries followed the soldiers and they brought with them many new ideas and many new ways.

Someone told Juan about Jesus. Juan came to know and love Jesus. He was baptized and walked every day to Mass. Juan loved Jesus, but he did not always like the Spanish! They conquered the Aztec people and enslaved them. Many died. The Aztec people were told that they were lowly in the eyes of their Spanish rulers.

Juan might have wondered at the words of a prayer he learned. It was the prayer Mary prayed when the angel brought her the news that she would bear Jesus. She praised God and said: **"I delight in God my savior, who regarded my humble state. The mighty arm of God scatters the proud in their conceit, pulls tyrants from their thrones, and raises up the humble."**

Mary, the Mother of God, called herself humble! And she herself told us that God raises up the humble.

December 9, 1531, began like any other day for Juan. He got up early and began walking to church. As Juan walked over a hill, he heard a voice calling his name. It was a woman's voice, and she was speaking not in Spanish, but in his Nahuatl language. When Juan looked around, he saw a young Aztec woman standing before him. Her skin was dark and she was dressed in the clothes of his people. She was wrapped with the sash that pregnant women wear. She was expecting a child.

The woman told Juan to go to the bishop and tell him, "You are to build a church on this hill." Juan must have been surprised, because the hill she meant was a holy place for the Aztec people, not for the Spanish. But Juan went to the bishop and said everything just as the woman had instructed.

The bishop listened and told Juan, "No. There will be no church on that hill." Perhaps he also knew that the hill was an Aztec holy place.

Again, Juan saw the Aztec woman. He asked, "Who are you?" She answered, "I am Mary, the Mother of God." And she told him to return to the bishop.

Juan went again to the bishop. He recounted all that the Mother of God had said. The bishop wondered just who Juan Diego was. He was only a farmer, a man of little learning and no power. He was an Aztec. Why should the bishop believe him?

Juan left, discouraged. It was now December 12. Three days had passed since he first saw the woman! What more could he do? He was walking home when Mary appeared again. This time the beautiful Aztec woman was surrounded by rose bushes, heavy with blossoms. Deep, blood-red roses, roses yellow as the summer sun, roses white as the snow — they lay at Mary's feet. Roses in December! Who could imagine such a thing? Roses in December! Who could make them bloom at such an unlikely time of year?

Mary told Juan to gather the roses in his cloak and take them to the bishop. Juan ran with his cloak filled with flowers.

The bishop was probably irritated to see Juan again. How many times did this stubborn man have to be told "no"? But the bishop's irritation turned to amazement when Juan opened his rough cloak to present the flowers. And there was something even more wonderful to see than roses in December.

There, on the rough cloth of the poor man's cloak, was imprinted an image of the Mother of God as she had appeared to Juan. The humble one whom God had raised to greatness had indeed appeared to the humble Juan Diego.

Lucy the Stubborn Teenager

About 1700 years ago, Lucy was born on Sicily, an island off the southwest coast of Italy. Lucy's parents were Christians, even though it was against the law to worship any gods but those of the Roman emperor. Like parents in all times and in all places, Lucy's mother and father worried about her. Would she suffer because her parents followed Christ?

In those days, parents chose husbands and wives for their children. Lucy's parents decided she should marry a certain man who worshiped the gods of the emperor, a powerful man who was a friend of the local governor.

But Lucy did not want to marry anyone. She wanted to devote herself to Christ by serving the poor.

Lucy's mother became very ill. She prayed for healing to Saint Agatha. Agatha had also lived in Sicily, and so was a favorite saint among the Christians there. Lucy's mother recovered from her sickness and wanted to show God her gratitude. She gave her daughter permission not to marry. She said, "Go and care for the poor as Christ has called you."

Lucy's fiancé was angry. The man wanted a wife! He was so angry that he went to the governor and denounced Lucy as a Christian.

The governor sent soldiers to arrest Lucy. They came into her house and ordered her out. She didn't move. So the soldiers decided to carry her out. They surrounded Lucy and tried to pick her up. It should have been easy: There were many soldiers and only one Lucy. But they could not move her!

The soldiers hitched Lucy to a team of oxen and ordered the team to move.

The oxen pulled and pulled, but Lucy did no

The soldiers decided to burn Lucy out. They poured hot oil on her and set her on fire, but she would not move. Nor did she die. One of the officers cried out, "Why don't you burn?" Lucy answered him, "To bear witness to my true bridegroom, Jesus Christ, I do not burn."

Finally, a scared and angry soldier ran a sword through Lucy's throat and she died. Like Saint Agatha before her, she was faithful to Christ in life and in death. Saint Lucy, whose name means "light," is celebrated to this day as a shining light in the darkness of Advent.

budge!

 Hagar Had a Baby

God had promised that Abram and his wife Sarah would have a child. But Abram was old, and Sarah was old, and they were tired of waiting for God. So Sarah suggested that her slave, Hagar, live for a time with Abram as a wife lives with her husband.

Hagar was young, and Sarah hoped she would conceive a child with Abram. Sarah planned to raise the child as her own, because, in Sarah's day, a childless wife lived in shame.

Hagar became pregnant. She was proud of carrying Abram's child. She stopped acting like Sarah's slave and began acting like Sarah's owner. Hagar might have refused to work. She might have begun demanding that Sarah fetch and carry for her. Maybe she said, "Oh, Sarah, my back hurts and my feet are tired. You cook dinner while I put my feet up."

Sarah was angry. She went to Abram and cried, "This is all your fault! Ever since she became pregnant, Hagar looks on me with disdain."

Now in those days, people did not understand that it is terribly wrong to own other human beings. So Abram simply said to Sarah, "Hagar is your slave. She is your property. Do whatever you want with her."

Sarah began to abuse Hagar. Maybe she called her names. Maybe she struck her. Whatever Sarah did, it was enough to make Hagar run away.

Hagar escaped into the wilderness. It was there, by a spring in the desert, that the Lord found Hagar. The Lord said, "Hagar, where have you come from, and where are you going?"

Hagar told the truth. She said, "I am running away from Sarah."

The Lord had hard words for Hagar, "Go back to Sarah and let her treat you badly." How frightened Hagar must have been! Then the Lord had encouraging words for Hagar,

"You shall bear a son,
you shall name him Ishmael,
for the Lord has heard you,
God has heard you."

But the Lord also had strange words for Hagar,

"He shall be a wild ass of a man,
his hand against everyone,
and everyone's hand against him."

Hagar was amazed. She asked herself, "Have I really seen God and remained alive after my vision?" Then she went back to Sarah and Abram. She gave birth and named the baby Ishmael, a Hebrew word meaning "God hears."

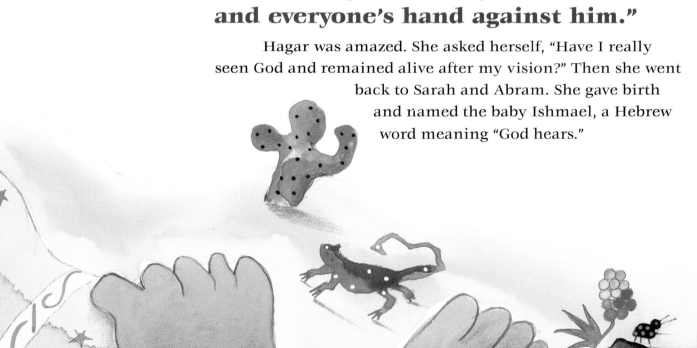

Sarah Had a Baby

Abraham and Sarah were old. They had lived together as husband and wife for many years. It had been their hope to have and raise children, but the years passed and Sarah did not conceive a child.

The story is told that Abraham felt sorry for a man named Abimelech, who, with his wife, also wanted children. Abraham prayed that "Abimelech and his house may multiply and increase." And they did! Abimelech's wife gave birth to a baby.

When the angels saw that Abraham's prayer for Abimelech had been answered, they cried out to God, "O Lord of the world! All these years Sarah has wanted a child, just as the wife of Abimelech wanted a child. Then Abraham prayed to you on her behalf, and you heard his prayer. Hear now our prayer for Sarah. It is right and just that Sarah should be remembered and granted a child."

According to this story, the angels prayed that prayer on the first day of the Jewish New Year, and about seven and a half months later, on the first day of the Jewish feast of Passover, Sarah gave birth to a son. She and

Abraham named him Isaac, a name that means "laughter."
They gave their son such a curious name because Sarah had
laughed when three visitors to their home prophesied that
she would have a child.

She laughed at the thought of an old woman and an old man having a baby.

But as this story is told among the Jews, many
other women also laughed with delight on that day when
Sarah laughed. God remembered all the women who
wanted a baby, just as God remembered Sarah. All these
women gave birth at Passover to children. And that
was not all: The eyes of the blind and the ears of the deaf
were opened, the mouths of the mute sang songs and the
limbs of the lame danced for joy.

Even the sun, on the happy day of Isaac's birth, shone
with a brightness the earth had not seen since Adam and
Eve lived in their beautiful garden home called paradise.

A Woman of Zorah Had a aby

Terrible times had come upon Israel. The people were ruled by their enemies, the Philistines. Terrible times had also come upon a woman and her husband from the town of Zorah. They wanted very badly to have children, but they could not.

One day, an angel of the Lord came to the woman. The angel said, "You will conceive and bear a son." Then the angel gave her this warning, "Be careful. Drink no wine, and eat no unclean food." And then the angel gave her news of the child she had not yet conceived:

"As for your son, no razor shall touch his head. His hair shall be a sign that this child is to be consecrated to God from the womb.

For it is he who will begin the deliverance of Israel from the Philistines."

The woman went at once and told her husband the strange and wonderful words of the angel. Her husband prayed, "O Lord, please send your angel to us again. We want to learn how we should raise our son."

The Lord heard his prayer, and the angel of the Lord came once again to the woman as she was sitting in the field. When she saw the angel, she ran and got her husband. He had many questions for the angel, and he wanted to hear for himself all that the angel had told his wife.

It was as if the man and woman could not believe that they would finally have a child—and they wanted to do everything right! They wanted to know the angel's name. The angel asked, "Why do you ask my name, which is mysterious? Why do you ask that which you cannot understand?" Then they wanted to serve dinner to the angel. The angel suggested they offer the food to God instead.

So the man and the woman kindled a fire on a stone altar, and they set fire to their food to offer it to God. The flames rose high, and as they watched, the angel of the Lord rose in the flames, up to heaven.

Up until that moment, the man and the woman weren't sure that they really had been speaking to an angel, but now they knew for certain. They were terrified and fell face down on the ground. When they dared to look up, the man said, "Now we will surely die, for we have seen God."

But the woman told her husband that if God wanted them dead, they never would have been told such good news. And the woman was right. She bore a son and named him Samson. The boy grew up and the Lord blessed him.

December 17

Lazarus' Tombs

Mary and Martha
and their brother, Lazarus,
were good friends of Jesus.
So when Lazarus became ill, his
sisters sent word to Jesus. They
wanted him to hurry to Bethany,
the town where Lazarus lived.

      By the time Jesus arrived,
Lazarus had been dead for four days.
Mary and Martha did not understand why it had
taken Jesus so long to come from Jerusalem to Bethany.
Jerusalem was only about two miles from their home.
Mary didn't even go out to greet Jesus when he neared the village.
Perhaps she was angry. Martha greeted Jesus alone, and she said
what many of their friends were saying, "Lord, if you had been here,
my brother would not have died." Then she added, "But even now I know
that whatever you ask of God, God will give you."

Jesus said something strange to Martha. He said, "Your brother will rise."

Martha thought Jesus was talking about the resurrection of the dead at the end of time. But Jesus meant that Lazarus would rise from the dead now, on this very day. Jesus explained this to Martha and asked her, "Do you believe this?"

Martha answered, "Yes, Lord. I believe that you are the Messiah, the Son of God."

Jesus and all the mourners went to the tomb where Lazarus lay. The tomb was a cave, with a big stone rolled across the opening. Jesus stood there and wept for his friend.

Then Jesus said to Martha, "Take away the stone."

Martha did not want to roll away the stone. She knew Lazarus's body would have begun to decay. She knew Lazarus's decaying body would stink. Still, Martha did as Jesus asked.

Jesus raised his eyes to heaven and began to pray. "Father, I thank you for hearing me." And then Jesus called, "Lazarus, come out!"

Lazarus stood up and walked out of the tomb! He was still wrapped tightly in his burial cloth, but he was walking. He was alive!

What happened then? People wonder about Lazarus's second life after his first life, and many stories are told about Lazarus's second life. One story tells that Lazarus and his sisters were at Jaffa, a seaport in Israel, where their enemies put them in a leaking boat. Their enemies hoped they would drown, but perhaps they didn't know how hard it was to kill Lazarus! God saved them again, and the three siblings landed safely on the island of Cyprus. The story says that Lazarus settled there and became the bishop and lived peacefully on Cyprus for 30 years.

Another story is like the first, but in this one, Lazarus's enemies put his sisters and him in a boat with no oars or rudder. The boat wouldn't sink, but neither could it be steered.

Lazarus's enemies hoped they would crash against the rocks or float into a storm.

But they landed safely on the coast of the country we now call France.

Lazarus became the bishop of Marseilles, a town in southern France. The story goes on to tell that Lazarus died there, not at all peacefully, but as a martyr who refused to worship the gods of the Roman empire.

However he died, Lazarus is the only human ever to have died and been buried twice! The people of a French town called Autun say that Lazarus's remains are buried in their cathedral.

They say you can go to Autun and check that Lazarus's body is still in the tomb.

annah Had a Baby

Long after the days of Sarah and Abraham, in the time of the judges, a woman named Hannah lived in Israel. She had never met Sarah, of course, but she had heard how God remembered Sarah and gave her a child. This story must have saddened Hannah, who also wanted a child, for she felt as though God had forgotten her!

Sarah and Abraham could share their longing for a child, but Hannah had no one to share her longing. Hannah's husband Elkanah had two wives: One was Hannah and the other was a woman named Peninnah. Elkanah and Peninnah already had many children. So Elkanah wasn't longing for a child. Peninnah wasn't longing for a child. Only Hannah longed for a child, and no one understood her sorrow. Peninnah teased her and called her cruel names.

Elkanah, who loved Hannah very much, wondered why she wasn't satisfied with his affection. He said, "Hannah, why do you weep, and why do you refuse to eat? Why do you grieve? Am I not more to you than ten children?"

All alone, Hannah went to the temple in Shiloh to ask God for a child. She prayed very quietly, "O Lord of hosts, look with pity on my misery. Remember me; do not forget me! Give me a son, and I will give him to the Lord for as long as he lives."

A priest in the temple named Eli saw Hannah moving her mouth and crying, but he could not hear her prayer. He thought she was drunk.

Hannah did look strange. To see how strange she looked, stand in front of a mirror and move your mouth to make word shapes without any sound. It looks crazy.

Eli was angry to have this strange woman in the temple, and he said, "How long will you make a drunken show of yourself? Sober up!"

Poor Hannah tried to explain. She said, "I am not drunk. I am unhappy, and I am pouring out my misery to God."

Eli then realized he had misjudged Hannah, and he said gently, "Go in peace, and may the God of Israel grant what you ask."

Hannah went home and discovered something wonderful. She was pregnant! God had remembered Hannah, and Hannah remembered God.

When the baby was born, she and Elkanah named him Samuel. "Samuel" means "name of God," and it sounds like another Hebrew name, "Saul," which means "to ask a favor."

As soon as Samuel was weaned, she took him to the temple in Shiloh, just as she had promised. Hannah left Samuel with the priest Eli and went alone to pray and sing:

**"I acclaim the Lord's greatness!
Only you are holy, Lord;
there is none but you."**

Elizabeth Had a Baby

Elizabeth was an old woman, and her husband Zechariah was an old man. All through their marriage they had wanted a child, but no child was born to them. Elizabeth and Zechariah were sad, but still they served God.

Zechariah was a priest in the temple in Jerusalem. One day it was his turn to go into the sanctuary in the temple to tend the fire that burned before the altar. Enormous clouds of sweet-smelling incense smoked on the fire. No one else was with Zechariah, so he was frightened to see someone appear in the smoke that billowed from the fire.

Who could it be? It was the angel of the Lord, the angel Gabriel.

The angel said, "Do not be afraid, Zechariah. God has heard your prayers. Elizabeth will conceive and bear a child, a son. You shall name him John. And you and your family and friends will rejoice at John's birth, for he will be great in the sight of the Lord." Now Zechariah knew the ways of nature. He knew that Elizabeth was too old to bear a child. Gabriel's words made no sense, and he told the angel so!

Gabriel did not argue. The angel simply said, "I was sent to bring you good news, but because you do not believe me, you will be unable to speak a word until my words are fulfilled."

Now the people praying outside the sanctuary began to wonder why Zechariah was taking so long. Had he fallen? Was he ill? When he finally came out, he couldn't speak. He couldn't tell them about Gabriel. He couldn't tell them what Gabriel promised.

But the people knew that something wonderful must have happened. They saw Zechariah's face, and they knew that he must have looked into heaven.

As for Zechariah, in silence he went home to Elizabeth. And there, just as the angel said, she conceived a child. Together, Elizabeth and Zechariah waited for their child to be born.

Nine months passed, and Elizabeth gave birth to a baby boy. Her family and friends rejoiced with her. They gathered for a party on the eighth day after the baby's birth. It was the day of his circumcision and of his naming. Elizabeth's friends and family all said, "Of course, you're going to name the baby Zechariah, after his father."

But Elizabeth said, "No. He will be named John."

Everyone began to protest. "There's no one in your family named John. No Uncle John, no Grandpa John, no Cousin John. You can't name him John!" And they turned to Zechariah, expecting him to agree.

Zechariah, who could hear but not speak, motioned for a tablet to write on. He wrote, "John is his name." Everyone but Elizabeth was amazed, and then something even more amazing happened. Zechariah's mouth opened and his tongue broke free. He began to speak, praising God,

"You, child, will be called Prophet of the Most High, for you will come to prepare a pathway for the Lord."

John grew up and became a great prophet. It was John who baptized Jesus.

Mary Had a Baby

Mary lived in a little town in Galilee called Nazareth. She was engaged to be married to a carpenter named Joseph. One day, the angel Gabriel came to Mary and greeted her, saying, "Hail, Mary. The Lord is with you."

Mary was afraid. She was not a powerful person in the community. The elders did not seek her advice on difficult matters. Why would an angel come to her? What sort of news might an angel bring? Mary feared that the angel's words might be something she didn't want to hear.

But the angel comforted her, "Do not be afraid, Mary. You have found favor with God. You will conceive and bear a child, a son. You shall name him Jesus. He will be great and will be called the Son of the Most High."

Now Mary was confused, and she told the angel so. She said, "How can I conceive and bear a child?" Mary knew that it was impossible for her to have a baby.

The angel told her, "Consider your cousin Elizabeth. She is an old woman, well past the age of child-bearing. Yet she, who never bore a child, is now in the sixth month of her pregnancy. Nothing is impossible for God."

Then Mary, who loved and served God all her days, praised God, saying, "Behold, I am the handmaid of the Lord. May it be done to me according to your word."

Mary may have been at peace with the startling news, but Joseph was not. When he heard that Mary was to bear a child, Joseph suspected that she had been living with another man the way a woman lives with her husband. So Joseph decided to release her quietly from their engagement.

Joseph made his decision at night and then he fell asleep. As he slept, the angel of the Lord appeared to him in a dream and said, "Joseph, do not be afraid to take Mary as your wife. It is through the Holy Spirit that this child has been conceived in her. She will bear a son and you are to name him Jesus."

When Joseph woke up, he went to see Mary. We don't know what he said to her, but he certainly needed to apologize for doubting her word. She had seen an angel, and now he had seen one, too!

Mary, who had so much to think about, left and went to the hill country of Judah to visit her cousin Elizabeth. When she reached the house, Mary called out a greeting. As soon as Elizabeth heard Mary's voice, the child within her womb leaped for joy. Elizabeth said to Mary, "Blessed are you among women, and blessed is the fruit of your womb! And blessed is she who trusted that the Lord's word to her would be fulfilled."

Mary praised God and said,

"Truly from this day on all ages will call me blest."

The cousins spent three months together, and then Mary returned home.

Thomas Builds a Palace

Long, long before Francis Xavier went to India, stories were told of the apostle Thomas and his days in India. Tradition has it that the apostles went all over the world revealing through their lives and their teachings the good news of Christ. And tradition also has it that Thomas went to India.

At first, Thomas didn't want to go there. He was a Jew. He was also a poor man with no education. He didn't want to go to a land where he could not speak the language, where he didn't know the customs of the people. Thomas didn't want to live as a stranger. He said "no" to India.

Then Christ appeared in a vision to an Indian man named Abban. Abban was in Palestine on behalf of his master, a prince of India. Christ told Abban, "Thomas is yours. He is India's. I give him to you."

When Abban approached Thomas and told him the story of the vision, Thomas understood. He knew, "My life is not my own. I belong to Christ. Where he sends me I will go."

So Abban and Thomas set out on the long journey to India. They came to the palace of Abban's master, Prince Gundafor.

Gundafor asked Thomas, "What is your trade?" Thomas replied, "I am a carpenter and a builder. I can build anything. I can make plows and oars from wood. I can build tombs and palaces from stone."

Gundafor ordered Thomas to build him a palace, and Thomas laid out the plans. There would be doors toward the east for light and windows toward the west for air. The king was well pleased with the plans. He left on a trip and told Thomas, "When I return, have my palace ready for me."

While Gundafor was gone, Thomas built nothing at all. He took the money for the palace and gave it to the poor. Every single penny!

When Gundafor returned he was furious to find a patch of bare earth where he expected to find a palace. He called for Thomas and shouted,

"Where is my palace?"

Thomas said, "It is finished. But you cannot see it here. You can only see it in heaven."

Gundafor thought Thomas was cheating him. He had Thomas arrested and imprisoned. He ordered him to be whipped to death.

Before Thomas could be executed, Gundafor's brother died. After his death, the brother appeared to Gundafor in a dream. He said, "Gundafor, Thomas has told you the truth! Your palace is finished, and it is in heaven, just as Thomas said."

So Gundafor awoke and went to the prison and released Thomas. He asked Thomas to baptize him, and they went together to the table of the eucharist. They went to the table not as employer and employee, not as master and servant, not as strangers from different lands and cultures, but as companions in faith.

No one knows when Thomas was born or when he died. The church in India keeps his feast on July 3, but for a long time, the rest of the world gave him this day so close to Christmas. It is the shortest day of the year in one part of the world, and the longest day in another part.

A Christmas Card from Prison

Dietrich Bonhoeffer was a young Lutheran pastor when Adolf Hitler and his Nazi party took control of Germany in the 1930s. Like King Herod, whose story you will soon read, Hitler set out to kill or imprison anyone who threatened his great power. Like King Henry II, whose story is told just after Herod's, Hitler believed that people should be his servants first, not God's. But pastor Bonhoeffer was God's faithful servant, and he opposed anyone who would try to take God's place. Pastor Bonhoeffer was one of the men and women who worked to rid Germany of Hitler.

Many people, millions of people, were imprisoned during Hitler's cruel reign. Some, like the Jews and the Gypsies, the mentally retarded and the mentally ill, were rounded up and put into concentration camps simply because of who they were. Nearly all of these innocent people were put to death.

The police also arrested and imprisoned anyone who dared to speak out or work against Hitler and the Nazi government. Many of these courageous people were put to death.

Pastor Bonhoeffer was sent to prison in 1943. During his time in prison he wrote letters to his family and his friends. He wrote to his parents in the last days of Advent 1943, remembering all the lovely Christmas celebrations of the past. He thanked them "for making Christmas so beautiful." But he spoke of the beauty of that prison Christmas, too, for his cell was much more like the stable where Jesus was born than any of the warm, comfortable houses he had known. Like Saint Andrew thanking his captors for allowing him to die like Jesus, Bonhoeffer thanked God that he could share his cold, bare place with Jesus. Bonhoeffer wrote to his mother and father:

For a Christian there is nothing particularly difficult about Christmas in a prison cell. I dare say it will have more meaning and be observed with greater sincerity here in this prison than in places where all that survives of the feast is its name. That misery, suffering, poverty, loneliness, helplessness and guilt look very different to the eyes of God from what they do to us, that God should come down to the very place which people usually abhor, that Christ was born in a stable because there was no room for him in the inn —— these are things which a prisoner can understand better than anyone else. For the prisoner the Christmas story is glad tidings in a very real sense. And that faith gives the prisoner a part in the communion of saints . . .

Pastor Bonhoeffer kept one more Christmas in prison.
Then, on April 9, 1945, he was called from the prayer service
he had been leading for his fellow prisoners. He turned to
one of them and said, "This is the end; for me, the beginning
of life." The next day, Bonhoeffer and five other prisoners
were hanged.

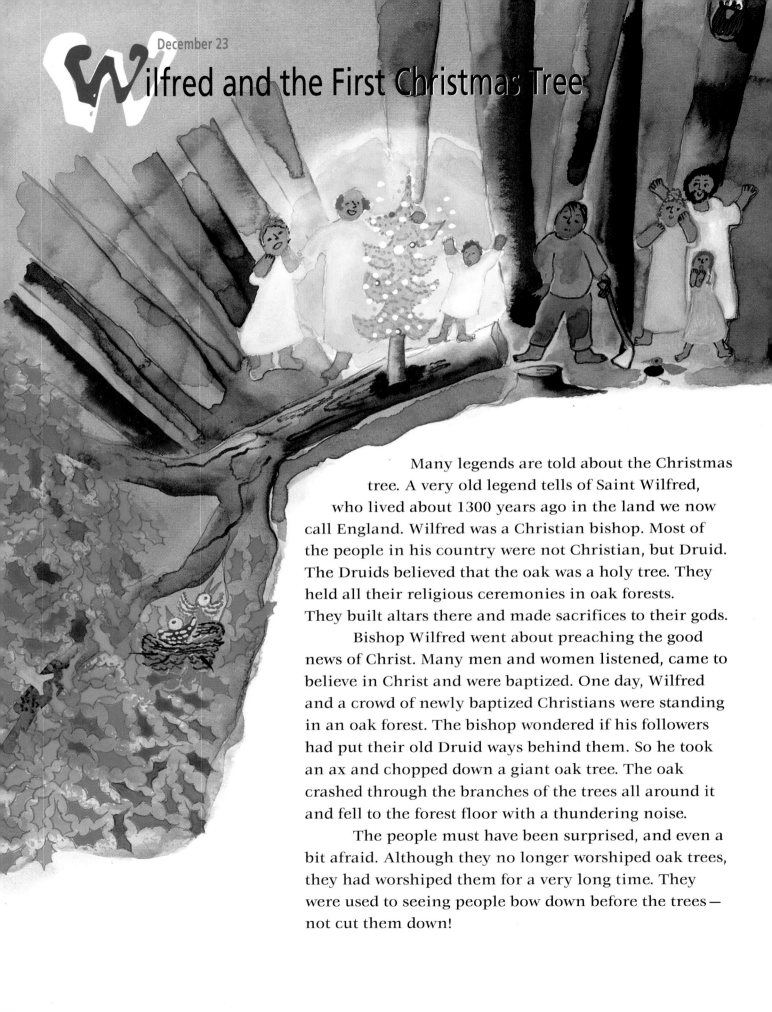

Wilfred and the First Christmas Tree

Many legends are told about the Christmas tree. A very old legend tells of Saint Wilfred, who lived about 1300 years ago in the land we now call England. Wilfred was a Christian bishop. Most of the people in his country were not Christian, but Druid. The Druids believed that the oak was a holy tree. They held all their religious ceremonies in oak forests. They built altars there and made sacrifices to their gods.

Bishop Wilfred went about preaching the good news of Christ. Many men and women listened, came to believe in Christ and were baptized. One day, Wilfred and a crowd of newly baptized Christians were standing in an oak forest. The bishop wondered if his followers had put their old Druid ways behind them. So he took an ax and chopped down a giant oak tree. The oak crashed through the branches of the trees all around it and fell to the forest floor with a thundering noise.

The people must have been surprised, and even a bit afraid. Although they no longer worshiped oak trees, they had worshiped them for a very long time. They were used to seeing people bow down before the trees — not cut them down!

As the puzzled crowd watched, the fallen oak split into four pieces. One piece fell to the north, one fell to the south, one fell to the east and one fell to the west. From the center of the stump a young fir tree began to rise. Wilfred put down the ax and spoke to the wondering people. He said,

"This tree shall be our holy tree.
   It is the wood of peace,
for our houses are built of fir.
   It is the sign of eternal life,
for its leaves are evergreen.
   Its branches grow in the shape of the cross
to remind us that Jesus gave us life from the cross.
   Its spire points to heaven,
as Jesus points the way to heaven.
   We will call it the tree of the Christ Child.
We will not gather about this tree in the wild woods,
but in our homes.
   This tree will not shelter spilled blood.
   This tree will shelter only our loving gifts
and our acts of kindness."

The Great–Great–Great–Great–Great–Grandparents

We get used to the smells and sounds of our apartment or house. We learn how to find the light switch even in the dark. We know the best places to hide presents and the warmest spot by the radiator. We discover just what combination of jiggle and push will open a stuck door or drawer. We remember who in the neighborhood gives out big candy bars on Halloween and whose dogs are friendly.

So just imagine how sad and confused Adam and Eve must have been to leave their home in the garden. They knew the names of every flower, every bush and every tree. They lived in peace among birds and bugs and fish, among animals that crept on the ground and that leapt through the trees.

Adam and Eve never had to work in the garden. Their job was to enjoy it, to eat its ripe fruit and to drink its fresh water. They never had to shovel snow or run through a hailstorm. They never had to bail water out of a flooded basement. They only had to gaze with joy on all that God had made. It was a very good life.

Many more stories are told about Adam and Eve than the ones we have in the Bible. One story tells of a weeping Adam and a weeping Eve, unwilling to leave the garden with empty hands. They wanted to take something with them, as we might bring home a souvenir to remind us of a wonderful trip. So Adam and Eve cut off a branch from the Tree of Life and carried it with them out of the garden.

When they reached their new home outside the garden, Adam and Eve planted the branch. It took root and began to grow. The tree grew, but it never flowered or set fruit. In fact, it never even leafed out. For hundreds of years, tall, bare limbs reached to the sky. No family ever picnicked in its shade. No child ever hid in its cool, green depths. People must have told stories about the strange old tree that looked dead but somehow stayed alive.

One day a baby was born in Bethlehem, in Judea. The baby was Jesus, Christ the Lord, the one who had been promised to the world for so long.

And on that day, the tree burst into bloom and bore fruit.

The tree flourished in its place for many years. It flourished until the day that soldiers came and cut the tree down. They split the ancient tree into logs. They nailed the logs together to make a cross, a cross for Jesus. Maybe that is why, on the day before Christmas, we remember the ones who started it all, our great-great-great-great-great-great grandparents, Adam and Eve.

Birth of the Lord

And it came to pass in those days that there went out a decree from Caesar Augustus that all the world should be taxed. And all went to be taxed, everyone into his own city. And Joseph also went up from Galilee, out of the city of Nazareth, into Judea, unto the city of David, which is called Bethlehem (because he was of the house and lineage of David), to be taxed with Mary, his espoused wife, being great with child.

And so it was that, while they were there, the days were accomplished that she should be delivered. And she brought forth her firstborn son, and wrapped him in swaddling clothes, and laid him in a manger, because there was no room for them in the inn.

And there were in the same country shepherds abiding in the fields, keeping watch over their flocks by night. And, lo, the angel of the Lord came upon them, and the glory of the Lord shone round about them; and they were sore afraid.

And the angel said unto them,

"Fear not; for behold, I bring you good tidings of great joy, which shall be to all people. For unto you is born this day in the city of David a savior, which is Christ the Lord.

And this shall be a sign unto you: you shall find the babe wrapped in swaddling clothes, lying in a manger."

And suddenly there was with the angel a multitude of the heavenly host, praising God and saying,

"Glory to God in the highest, and on earth peace, good will toward all."

Stephen the First Martyr

You might think that the day after we hear the story of Jesus' birth, we would hear stories about his childhood friends and about their play together in Nazareth. But the stories that begin today tell of the cost of being Jesus' companion on the journey, the cost of being one of the *comites Christi,* the companions of Christ.

Stephen was a member of the very first Christian church in Jerusalem. The leaders of the church were the apostles of Christ, people who had walked and worked with Jesus. As the community grew, the apostles found that they were not able to take good care of all the members. The apostles were supposed to pray, preach and teach. But there was so much else to do. Some widows needed food. Sick people waited and waited for a brother or sister to come and change their bandages or treat their cuts. Prisoners sat alone in jail, hoping to hear news of their families and friends, longing for a kind word.

The apostles needed plenty of help to care for the daily needs of the people of the church! So they gathered the whole community together and asked them to choose seven members, members who loved God and who followed God in all things. The deacons would be like servants to the poor and needy.

These seven would be called deacons, a word which means "servant."

Stephen, whose name in Greek means "crown," was one of the original seven deacons. His crown was the sick and hungry and ill and lonely of the church. He tended them with care and joy. The scripture says that Stephen was "full of grace and fortitude" and that he "did great wonders and signs among the people."

We don't know what Stephen's "signs and wonders" were, but they certainly caught the attention of the town leaders who didn't trust the church. During Stephen's life, it was against the law to believe that Jesus is the Son of God, the Christ. So Stephen was arrested and brought before the judges.

Many people gathered for Stephen's trial. They were his enemies, and they raged against him. Stephen did not look at the hateful crowd—surely it was too scary! Instead he looked up to heaven.

Stephen stood looking up for a long time. At last, he saw the heavens open, and he saw the whole glory of God. Then Stephen saw Jesus standing at the right hand of God. He cried out in wonder at what he saw.

When the mob heard Stephen cry, "Behold, I see the heavens opened," they fell upon him. They dragged Stephen outside the city gates and dumped him there. The crowd scurried about, picking up large stones, lots of them, gathering them into a pile.

People began throwing stones at Stephen. He cried to God, "Lord Jesus, receive my spirit."

Then Stephen cried again to God, asking for his killers to be forgiven. He cried, "Lord, lay not this sin to their charge." And with those words, Stephen died, the first of Christ's companions to die for the faith.

Old John the Apostle

Jesus called John and his brother James "the sons of thunder." Perhaps that's because they would get angry and storm and thunder at those around them. One time John and James got so angry that they asked Jesus to throw down fire from heaven on the people they were angry with. But Jesus refused.

In the gospel that bears John's name, we learn more about Jesus' love and close friendships than we do in any of the other gospels. We hear of Jesus celebrating with his friends at a wedding. We hear of Jesus weeping with his friends Mary and Martha when Lazarus died. We hear Jesus say to his followers: "No longer do I call you servants, for the servant does not know what the master is doing; but I have called you friends."

In John's gospel we hear about Jesus' very best friend on earth, called "the beloved disciple." When Jesus hung dying on the cross, he asked the beloved disciple to care for

Mary as though she were his own mother. Then Jesus asked Mary to care for the disciple as though he were her own child. The name of the beloved disciple is never mentioned in the gospel, but many people think he is the apostle John.

Another book in the Bible is called the Acts of the Apostles. The stories in this book took place after the death and resurrection of Jesus, when Jesus sent the Holy Spirit to guide the apostles. There's a story about a time John and Peter went to the temple in Jerusalem and prayed that God would heal a crippled man. The man was healed, but John and Peter were arrested by the Roman authorities and taken to jail. They were told never again to preach the good news of Christ. John and Peter said, "We must tell the truth about the things we have seen and heard."

The Bible doesn't tell us what happened to John, but there is a very old story that John left Jerusalem and went to a city called Ephesus, where he was the bishop. Once again the Roman authorities arrested him. This time they banished him to an island called Patmos. After he was released, he returned to Ephesus.

John must have been the favorite preacher of the children of Ephesus, because he was famous for his short homilies! Saint Jerome writes that John, who was by that time very old and weak, would be carried into the church to preach. This was his homily Sunday after Sunday:

"My little children, love one another."

Some people—perhaps the ones who like long homilies—asked John why he couldn't say something else. "We're tired of hearing the same lesson over and over," they complained.

John listened. He thought the idea of another lesson was good. "But first," he said, "We have to learn this one."

King Herod and the Innocents

When Jesus was born in the land of Judah some 2000 years ago, a wicked king sat on the throne. The king's name was Herod, and he thought being king made him the most important person in the world. When he told people to do something, they did it! Herod meant to be king forever.

So Herod was disturbed by the news some astrologers from a faraway country brought to him. They had followed a star, they told Herod. They were looking for a child, a boy who would grow up and become a great king. They said, "The star is a sign. When we find the star, we will find the child." The child was Jesus.

Herod said, "I would like to find this child, too." Then he lied to his guests. He said, "I want to honor him."

Herod did not want to honor Jesus. He wanted to find the child and kill him before he could grow up and become a great king.

So he told the visitors, "When you find this child, come and tell me where he lives." And the astrologers from a faraway country agreed to do as Herod asked.

The visitors set out again, following the star that went before them. The star stopped over Bethlehem, and there the astrologers found Jesus and Mary and Joseph. They planned to go and tell Herod all about their journey, but they were warned by an angel in a dream to go home another way.

Joseph also was dreaming. In one dream, an angel appeared to Joseph and warned him to take Mary and Jesus to Egypt. The angel said, "Herod is searching for the child to kill him." Joseph woke at once and woke Mary, too. They wrapped up their baby and left that very night for Egypt!

When Herod realized that the astrologers weren't coming back, he fell into a rage. He ordered the murder of every boy in Bethlehem two years old and younger! Herod wanted to be sure this king-to-be was dead.

The soldiers of the king went from house to house doing the evil work of Herod. Mothers and fathers must have tried desperately to hide their babies. They must have pleaded with the soldiers to take them instead of their sons.

The whole land was filled with the sound of their cries.

Jesus was safe in Egypt, but many children died. Herod, the wicked king, had no mercy on any of them.

Thomas Becket Opens the Door

Nearly 900 years ago, Thomas Becket was born in England. He grew up and became the best friend of the king, Henry II. Henry loved being with Thomas, and he valued his advice. When Thomas was 36 years old, Henry appointed him chancellor, which means that Thomas was Henry's closest advisor. Henry wanted his friend nearby so that they could work together. They also loved to play sports and games together.

Then the Archbishop of Canterbury, the most important bishop in England, died. Henry decided to give Thomas the assignment. Being bishop was a higher position than being chancellor. Thomas wasn't a priest (he was a deacon), and he did not want to be a bishop. But Henry insisted, and then the pope, Alexander III, also insisted, and Thomas at last agreed to be ordained and appointed bishop. King Henry thought life would go on as before.

Thomas set out to become a good bishop, and he no longer had time for games. He began to dress simply, like a servant rather than a master. He began to rise early each morning to study the scriptures. He went out every day to distribute food and money among the needy people of his town. He was the most generous bishop the people of Canterbury could remember.

Thomas took special care that all who were appointed to lead the church were worthy of their duties. He did not seem to notice if the people appointed were rich and powerful or poor and powerless. He simply wanted honorable priests for the church.

King Henry had hoped Thomas would be a wise archbishop, but he didn't want him taking his job so seriously. He wanted Thomas to be a friend first and a bishop second. At last, King Henry grew angry with Thomas for choosing the good of the church over the good of the king.

The king was no longer Thomas' friend. In fact, he became his enemy. He sent Thomas away into exile. He took away land and money from Thomas. But Thomas would not stop being a good and faithful bishop.

King Henry complained bitterly about Thomas to some of his knights. The knights decided to kill Archbishop Thomas.

Thomas received a letter warning him of danger. Still, on December 29 in the year 1170, he went as usual to the church, carrying his cross before him. Three knights were waiting for him. Monks shut the heavy doors of the church against them, but Thomas walked over and let his killers come in. **The knights shouted, "Where is Thomas the traitor?" Thomas answered, "Here I am, no traitor, but archbishop and priest of God."**

The knights began to strike Thomas with their swords. Forced to his knees, Thomas murmured, "For the name of Jesus and in defense of the church, I am willing to die."

Soon the steadfast bishop lay still. He was dead, his body stretched out on the floor of the church. In later years and even today many people travel on pilgrimage to Canterbury and pray in the church where Bishop Thomas died.

How We Name the Days

Do you remember when you lost your first tooth? Do you remember the first time you rode a two-wheeler by yourself? Maybe you're still waiting for these things to happen. When you lose your baby teeth or learn to ride a bike, you start to think of time as "before" and "after." You might tell friends, "That was back when I rode a tricycle."

Life gets divided into different times: The crossing-the-street-holding-Dad's-hand years are not the crossing-the-street-by-myself years. Sledding-on-the-hill days are not swimming-in-the-lake days.

All people divide time. We divide daylight from darkness and special occasions from usual routines. We give these divisions names. We call the light "day" and the darkness "night." We call special occasions names such as "birthdays" and "anniversaries."

More complicated ways to divide time are "weeks" and "months" and "years." If you watch the moon every night you will see that it changes over a period of around 29 days, which is about a month. That's how long it takes for the full moon to grow smaller and smaller, then larger and larger until it becomes a full moon again. The very first calendars probably were based on watching the moon.

Long ago, the Romans began naming the months, and many modern people have kept the names. We call the first month "January," a word taken from the name of the Roman god Janus, who ruled beginnings and endings. Drawings of Janus show him with two faces, one looking backward and one looking forward. Why is that a good name for the first month of the year? The name "April" perhaps was taken from the Roman word *aperire,* which means "to open." What opens in April?

People always have a "start-over day" when they celebrate a new year. And different people count the years differently. Muslims count the years from when the prophet Mohammed fled from the city of Mecca to the city of Medina. The Jewish New Year is said to be the anniversary of the creation. This day falls close to the autumn equinox, when day and night are of equal length. After all, when God created the world, day and night certainly must have been equal!

Christians begin their count of the years with the birth of Jesus. And during the days that we celebrate his birth, we end the old year and begin a new one.

We like to think that all our years, when we put them together, are different from the two-faced god Janus who keeps beginning and ending, beginning and ending, but going nowhere. And time really isn't like the moon, growing full and then growing dark, again and again. We like to think that time had a single beginning and will have a single ending—and what a wonderful ending it will be! Each year brings us closer to Christ and to the eternity that we were promised.

Wise Melania

Melania (whose name means "black" and rhymes with "bella mia") was a Christian woman who lived in Rome during the last days of the Roman empire. In her lifetime she saw governments crumble and worlds turned upside down. Some of those worlds Melania turned upside down by herself! She is a good saint for the dying of an old year and the beginning of a new, because she witnessed so many changes, so many dyings and rebirths.

Melania's family was very wealthy. They wanted her to marry a rich man, but she wanted to remain single so that she could better serve the poor. She would make the poor her family.

Melania's parents insisted, and, when she was just 14, she married a good man named Pinian, who was only 17. They had two children, both of whom died as infants. Through joy and sorrow, Melania and Pinian remained true to one another and to God. Pinian respected Melania and learned wisdom from her. The day came when he said,

"You are right. God is calling us to serve the poor."

Melania and Pinian owned much land and many slaves. They set all 8000 slaves free! Then they sold all their land and gave the money to the poor. But even more changes were coming. A tribe of people from the north, the Goths, invaded Rome. In the year 406, Melania and Pinian and Melania's mother fled Rome and the invaders. It was certainly easier for them to do this now than it would have been when they owned all that property and all those slaves. Imagine trying to get 8003 people out of town!

Melania and Pinian went to north Africa and settled down. There, Melania became a monk and a scholar. She established a monastery, where people lived together like sisters or brothers. She supported the monastery by writing books in Latin and in Greek.

After 11 years in north Africa, the three moved to Jerusalem, where yet more changes were to come. Melania became a hermit, living a life of prayer and solitude.

By the year 439, Melania's husband and mother had both died. That Christmas, Melania went to Bethlehem with friends. She knew she was dying, but after a lifetime in God's company, she was certainly not afraid of eternity there.

So on Sunday, December 31, she went to Mass. Her good friend Gerontius presided at the Mass. He, too, knew Melania was dying, and his voice was so choked with tears that people had trouble understanding his words, but understood his sadness. After Mass, Melania spent the day visiting with her friends. Finally, she lay down and said her last words, "As the Lord willed, so it is done." And so it was done, and so it had been done for all the years of that good and learned woman, Melania.

Escape into Egypt

After the angel warned them about King Herod's evil plan to kill the baby Jesus, Joseph and Mary took their son Jesus and fled to safety in Egypt. It was a long journey and a dangerous one. Perhaps they saw Herod's soldiers hunting the child. Perhaps they hid among trees and behind rocks as the soldiers passed by. Many tales are told of the help the three received from plants and animals along the way. Some of the help was bold, and some of the help was the expected kindness people gave to any strangers on the road. All of the stories are good to hear.

One story is told that Mary and Joseph heard the soldiers approaching. Mary was too tired to run, and Joseph would not leave her side. They looked

about and saw a towering pine tree, ancient and hollow. The old pine invited them to rest inside its empty trunk. The family hurried inside. Then the pine lowered its sweeping branches around its trunk, concealing Mary and Joseph and the baby Jesus from the soldier's sharp eyes. There the three slept safely, all through the night.

The story says that when morning came, Jesus raised his arms and blessed the faithful pine. Some say that if you cut a pine cone in half lengthwise, you can still see the imprint of Jesus' hand.

Another story tells of the Holy Family stopping to rest on a hillside. They were weary and hungry and dirty, too. Mary took all their clothes down to a nearby stream, and she cleaned them there. **There must have been lots of diapers to wash!**

She looked around for a place to hang the clothes to dry. Near the stream grew a sweet-smelling bush. Mary hung her laundry from its branches, and then the bush was rewarded for its service to her. God gave the bush blossoms colored the same blue as Mary's robe. And God gave the bush a name, rosemary, which it still shares with the Mother of God.

Basil and Gregory: Good Friends and Bishops

Basil and Gregory were born in the same year, 329, and in the same place, Asia Minor, the country now called Turkey. Basil's name means "royal" and Gregory's name means "watchful." They grew up to be dear friends, and they both worked as bishops.

Certainly another thing they had in common was the large number of holy people each counted in his family! Basil's father and mother, a grandmother, a sister and two brothers are all remembered as saints. Gregory's father and mother and sister and brother also are remembered as saints. It's as if sainthood was the family business!

The two men had a lot in common, but they were not much alike. Basil enjoyed being with people. He wrote that people "are gentle and sociable beings, and not solitary and savage. Nothing is as proper to our nature as to have need of one another."

Basil began a monastery organized as a community of people who worked together, and they also worked alongside the people of the city. The monastery had a school attached to it, and even an orphanage.

Gregory, though never savage, was often solitary. He longed to be alone in prayer with the Lord he loved and whom he called "my Christ." He certainly never wanted to be ordained a priest or appointed a bishop, but Gregory's goodness and learning drew people to him. Again and again Gregory was called to leave his joyful silence to serve the church.

When Gregory said that he wasn't happy about being a leader in the church, Basil accused Gregory of failing to do his duty. The two friends had a dreadful fight. Reluctantly Gregory gave in and traveled to one city or another to help the people.

He knew that he didn't look like anyone's idea of what a bishop should look like. His body was stooped, his head was bald, and he wore shabby clothes. It was only when people heard Gregory speak that they fully appreciated him, because he was wise and holy. People came from all around to hear Gregory's teaching, especially about the three persons in God, the Holy Trinity.

Basil wore his bishop's robes more easily than Gregory. Basil preached every morning and every evening to great crowds of people. He organized a soup kitchen. He took care that the hungry and poor were fed and clothed and housed. He gave away his own inheritance to those in need and built a large hospital for their care.

Basil preached,

"The bread in your cupboard belongs to the hungry person. The coat hanging unused in your closet belongs to the person who needs it. The shoes rotting in your closet belong to the person with no shoes. The money you put in the bank belongs to the poor. You do wrong to everyone you could help, but fail to help."

When Basil died, his friend Gregory preached at his funeral. How sad Gregory must have been to say goodbye to Basil. He asked Basil to welcome him one day into heaven. He hoped that the two of them, so often separated by their work in the church, would never again be parted.

What Anna and Simeon Knew

During Mary's time, a Jewish woman who gave birth to a son waited 40 days before making a sacrifice to give thanks to God. Following this custom, when Jesus was 40 days old, his mother Mary took him to the temple in Jerusalem. Joseph came with them. She and Joseph were going to present their baby son to God and offer God the thanksgiving sacrifice.

The temple was a busy place. Jews came there to pray — to thank God, to ask God for blessings and to listen to God. Jews came there to remember what it meant to be a Jew. They came to the temple to sit and walk and worship where their ancestors had sat and walked and worshiped. The temple was also a place where old people could sit in peace and quiet.

Mary and Joseph soon ran into two of these old people. Simeon was a very old man and Anna was a very old woman. They had been waiting in Jerusalem all their lives to see the Promised One of Israel. God had told Simeon that he wouldn't die until he saw the Promised One with his own eyes. On the day Mary arrived with Jesus, Simeon saw the baby, and he knew that God's promise had come true! The old man took the tiny child in his arms, and he blessed God, saying,

**"Lord, let your servant
die in peace,
for you kept your promise.
With my own eyes
I see the salvation
you prepared for all peoples:
a light of revelation for the Gentiles,
and glory to your people Israel."**

Anna was another prophet who stayed night and day in the temple, where she prayed and fasted. She was 84 years old. She had been a mother and a wife, as well as a prophet, and she was worn out. But Anna, too, wanted to see God's promises fulfilled.

When Anna saw Jesus, she blessed God just as Simeon had. Then she went and told the good news to all who, like herself, were waiting for God.

Elizabeth Ann Seton: Wife, Mother, Teacher, Saint

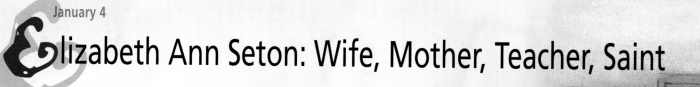

Elizabeth Ann Bayley was born in 1774, two years before the Declaration of Independence was written and signed. She grew up in New York City.

She liked to go with her father, a doctor, as he made his rounds. He was often called to the bedsides of poor immigrants who were sick and sometimes dying far from their homes. To be sick and a stranger in a strange land is a terrible thing. Elizabeth Ann herself came to know that.

Elizabeth Ann grew up trusting God. She trusted God in her marriage to William Seton and in the births of their five children. But her trust was tested. Her husband's business failed, and then he fell ill. There was little money in the house and little time for play, as Elizabeth Ann devoted herself to her husband's care. Still, she did not forget her children. When her husband was asleep or resting, Elizabeth Ann could be found jumping rope with the children.

She knew that children need to play and to laugh even in the saddest of times.

Elizabeth Ann's husband grew weaker. The doctor suggested taking him to Italy, where the sun is warm and the air is mild. So they made the long voyage and reached the docks of Livorno. There, Elizabeth Ann's husband died, far from home, a stranger in a strange land.

Elizabeth Ann was alone in Italy. She must have been afraid. Then a family welcomed her into their home. She saw that they lived what they prayed, and she was moved by their hospitality. She decided to join them in the Catholic church. She had always been a Christian, but Elizabeth Ann wanted to join the community that had received her with such affection

and understanding. On Ash Wednesday in 1805 she walked into Saint Peter's Basilica in Rome and knelt there, saying, "My God, here let me rest."

There would be little rest for Elizabeth Ann. When she and her children returned to New York, they lived in poverty. She was barely able to support them as a teacher, even though she was a very good teacher. Children liked her because she understood their lively natures. She wrote of herself that "rules (and) prudence . . . are dreadful walls to a burning soul wild as mine." She compared herself to "a fiery horse."

Word of her gifts in the classroom spread all over the country. Even the bishop of Maryland heard of her. He wrote and asked her to come south and to start a teaching community of women.

Elizabeth Ann Seton agreed. She packed up and moved her children into a ramshackle house in Emmitsburg, Maryland. The roof had so many holes that in the winter snow fell onto their beds as they slept! But Elizabeth Ann had a merry heart. She was doing work she loved, among people she loved, for the God she loved.

So when she wrote about her troubles (and she did), she compared them to the bites of flies and mosquitoes, which bother people but do not destroy them. She wrote, "Wrap the cloak round and never mind them. They can only penetrate the surface." She urged her friends to "remember the sure, the never failing protector we have. God will not divide your confidence."

Syncletia, Riches to Rags

Syncletia, whose name rhymes with "how be ya'," lived about 1600 years ago in the city of Alexandria in Egypt. She was a lucky baby. When she was born, the lives of the poor were very hard and most people were poor. But Syncletia's parents were wealthy and kind. She would have servants to do the tiring and unpleasant work of her household. She would have time to read or to go to parties or to learn to paint or to do whatever she fancied. She would never have to struggle to earn a living or to save money.

People in Alexandria even thought Syncletia's little sister was lucky. It was true that she had been born blind, but she would always have a life of comfort and ease. She would have the best doctors and the best care Egypt could offer.

The sisters' parents died and left them a fortune. Friends counseled Syncletia to marry a man whose fortune she could add to her own. That way the sisters would always be rich. And it is true that Syncletia wanted an abundant life, but her idea of abundance

was very different from that of her friends. She wanted an abundance of joy, an abundance of peace, an abundance of time with God.

Syncletia knew that huge amounts of money take time. She would have to invest some money and spend some on houses and farmland. She would have to keep careful watch so that no one stole from her. She would have no time for what she loved best!

So Syncletia and her sister made a decision. They gave all their money away to the poor of Alexandria. They moved into rooms lent to them by a relative, and they began to live a life of prayer. No doubt their relative was dismayed to find himself saddled with two homeless women!

Some of Syncletia's friends and family thought the sisters had chosen too hard a life. What would they do without servants and fine foods and well-tended gardens? Who could stand so much quiet? But Syncletia thought it curious that anyone would find their good life hard. Just look, she said, at what people do "to heap up riches and perishable goods! They venture among thieves and robbers. At sea they expose themselves to the fury of winds and waves. They suffer shipwrecks and all perils. They attempt all, dare all, hazard all." God never asked anything of Syncletia and her sister but their company.

Word of Syncletia's wisdom soon spread among the women of Alexandria. They would come to her, bringing their questions, their problems, their fears and their hopes. We don't know if they sat on pillows talking or if they sat together on the hard floor. Perhaps they walked by the seashore, or they drank tea and talked.

However it happened, many people came to Syncletia and learned from her.

She lived to be 80 years old, a very great age in those days. When Syncletia was dying, the friends who had gathered about her bed saw a light surround her. They heard Syncletia speak of beautiful visions that she alone could see. The holy woman who gave up everything for God died in the abundant goodness of God.

Epiphany

The wise ones watched the sky. Night after night, they gazed into the darkness. Stars moved in patterns like the colored pebbles inside a kaleidoscope. A turn of the earth and the bright pieces shifted, and a different pattern emerged. The stars moved west as the seasons moved, all of it in harmony with the movement of the world on which the wise ones stood silently and watched.

One night a new star shone, blazing like a bonfire just above the horizon. The wise ones watched and wondered, for they believed the stars revealed something of the mysteries of God. They knew they would have to watch the stars for many years to learn their secrets. They would have to learn the patterns. They had already learned which stars shone high in the summer sky and which shone high when winter came. But this star was different. And so they decided to leave their homes and follow the star. Perhaps when they stood in the place directly under where it shone, they would know. They would know the mystery of God.

The story goes that there were three of them, one named Caspar, one named Balthasar (rhymes with "Hal, the star!"), and one named Melchior (rhymes with "Belle, see more"). Perhaps there were others who came with them: students and friends, sisters and brothers. All who truly wanted to find the star would have come on the journey.

Each day when the sun rose they would stop to feed and water their weary animals. Then they would unroll their blankets on a soft patch of ground and lie down

to rest. With the setting sun the travelers would be up and on the move again. It was not a map or a road sign or someone's directions that guided them, but the star.

Once they did ask directions. They stopped at the palace of a king. Surely he saw the light in the east. Surely his sleep had been interrupted by the glow outside his window. But he seemed not to have noticed. He was curious, troubled by the wise ones' belief that this star brought news of another king's birth. But of the star he knew nothing.

The three must have wondered as they left the king's palace, "Why couldn't he see the star?"

"He could see us," one said.

Leaving the king, they walked and rode until they came to the place where the star seemed to hover in the sky like a mother bending over her sleeping infant. There they found a baby and his mother and his father, and they were silent.

**At your great Name, O Jesus, now
All knees must bend, all hearts must bow;
All things on earth with one accord,
Like those in heav'n, shall call you Lord.**

Advent Morning Prayer

We have been silent all through the night. Now we ask God to open our mouths in praise. As we say these words, we use our thumb to make the sign of the cross on our lips.

Lord, open my lips.
And my mouth shall proclaim your praise.

Hymn

O come, O come, Emmanuel,
And ransom captive Israel,
That mourns in lonely exile here
Until the Son of God appear.
    Rejoice, rejoice! Emmanuel
    Shall come to you, O Israel.

O come, O Dayspring from on high
And cheer us by your drawing nigh;
Disperse the gloomy clouds of night,
And death's dark shadow put to flight.
    Rejoice, rejoice! Emmanuel
    Shall come to you, O Israel.

O come, Desire of nations, bind
In one the hearts of humankind;
O bid our sad divisions cease,
And be for us our King of Peace.
    Rejoice, rejoice! Emmanuel
    Shall come to you, O Israel.

Psalm 85

During the first weeks of Advent, until December 16, recite this psalm.

I listen to God speaking:
"I, the Lord, speak peace,
peace to my faithful people
who turn their hearts to me."
Salvation is coming near,
glory is filling our land.

Love and fidelity embrace,
peace and justice kiss.
Fidelity sprouts from the earth,
justice leans down from heaven.

The Lord pours out riches,
our land springs to life.
Justice clears God's path,
justice points the way.

Psalm 85:9–14

Song of Zechariah

Beginning December 17, recite or sing the Song of Zechariah (see the story on December 19).

Praise the Lord, the God of Israel,
who shepherds the people
    and sets them free.

God raises from David's house
a child with power to save.
Through the holy prophets
God promised in ages past
to save us from enemy hands,
from the grip of all who hate us.

Out of God's deepest mercy
a dawn will come from on high,
light from those shadowed by death,
a guide for our feet on the way
    to peace.

Luke 1:68–75, 78–79

Scripture

See the calendar of readings on the last page of this book. Read the scripture now or at Evening Prayer. After the reading, have a time of silence. The story for the day could be read after this.

Lord's Prayer

Morning Prayer concludes with the Our Father.

Christmas Season Morning Prayer

*We have been silent all through the night. As we ask
God to open our mouths in praise, we make the sign of
the cross.*

God's holy day has dawned for us.
O come, let us adore!

Hymn

*Sing "O come, all ye faithful" or another familiar
Christmas song such as the following:*

Refrain
Go tell it on the mountain
Over the hills and ev'rywhere;
Go tell it on the mountain
That Jesus Christ is born!

1. While shepherds kept their watching
   O'er silent flocks by night,
   Behold throughout the heavens
   there shone a holy light.

2. The shepherds feared and trembled
   When lo! Above the earth
   Rang out the angel chorus
   That hailed our Savior's birth.

3. Down in a lowly manger
   The humble Christ was born,
   And God sent us salvation
   That blessed Christmas morn.

*Afro-American Spiritual: Adapt. by John W. Work, Jr.,
1871–1925, © Mrs. John W. Work, III.*

Psalm 96

A new song for the Lord!
Sing it and bless God's name,
everyone, everywhere!
Tell the whole world
God's triumph day to day,
God's glory, God's wonder.

Proclaim the Lord, you nations,
praise the glory of God's power,
praise the glory of God's name!
Bring gifts to the temple,
bow down, all the earth,
tremble in God's holy presence.

Tell the nations, "The Lord rules!"
As the firm earth is not swayed,
nothing can sway God's judgment.
Let heaven and earth be glad,
the sea and sea creatures roar,
the field and its beasts exult.

Then let the trees of the forest sing
before the coming of the Lord,
who comes to judge the nations,
to set the earth aright,
restoring the world to order.

Psalm 96:1–3, 7–13

Scripture

*See the calendar of readings on the last page of this
book. Read the scripture now or at Evening Prayer.
After the reading, have a time of silence. The story for
the day could be read after this.*

Lord's Prayer

Morning Prayer concludes with the Our Father.

Advent Evening Prayer

A candle or the Advent wreath is lit as we make the sign of the cross and say:

Light and peace in Jesus Christ our Lord.
Thanks be to God.

Hymn

Sing this Advent hymn to its own tune given here, or to another tune such as "Praise God from whom all blessings flow."

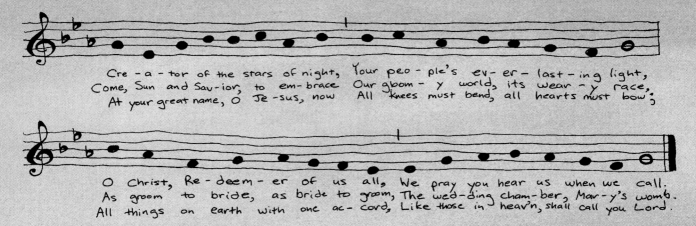

Cre - a - tor of the stars of night, Your peo - ple's ev - er - last - ing light,
Come, Sun and Sav - ior, to em - brace Our gloom - y world, its wear - y race,
At your great name, O Je - sus, now All knees must bend, all hearts must bow;

O Christ, Re - deem - er of us all, We pray you hear us when we call.
As groom to bride, as bride to groom, The wed - ding cham - ber, Mar - y's womb.
All things on earth with one ac - cord, Like those in heav'n, shall call you Lord.

Psalm 146

During the first weeks of Advent, until December 16, recite this psalm.

Praise the Lord, my heart!
My whole life, give praise.
Let me sing to God
as long as I live.
The Lord keeps faith for ever,
giving food to the hungry,
justice to the poor,
freedom to captives.

The Lord opens blind eyes
and straightens the bent,
comforting widows and orphans,
protecting the stranger.
The Lord loves the just
but blocks the path of the wicked.

Zion, praise the Lord!
Your God reigns for ever,
from generation to generation.
Hallelujah!

Psalm 146:1–2, 7–10

Song of Mary

Beginning December 17, recite or sing the Song of Mary.

I acclaim the greatness of the Lord,
I delight in God my savior,
who regarded my humble state.
Truly from this day on
all ages will call me blest.

For God, wonderful in power,
has used that strength for me.
Holy the name of the Lord!
Whose mercy embraces the faithful,
one generation to the next.

The mighty arm of God
scatters the proud in their conceit,
pulls tyrants from their thrones,
and raises up the humble.
The Lord fills the starving
and lets the rich go hungry.

God rescues lowly Israel,
recalling the promise of mercy,
the promise made to our ancestors,
to Abraham's heirs for ever.

Luke 1:46–55

Scripture

See the calendar of readings on the last page of this book. Read the scripture now or at morning prayer. After the reading, have a time of silence. The story for the day could be read after this.

Intercessions

At the end of the day we bring our needs before God. We pray for the world and all who are in need.

Lord's Prayer

After the Our Father, we seal our prayer with the greeting of peace. A candle or the Christmas tree is lit as we make the sign of the cross and say:

Blessed are you, Lord God of all creation.
You bring forth light from darkness.

Christmas Season Evening Prayer

Hymn

This Christmas song or another may be sung here.

Hark, the herald angels sing,
   "Glory to the newborn King!
Peace on earth and mercy mild,
   God and sinners reconciled!"
Joyful, all ye nations rise;
   Join the triumph of the skies;
With angelic hosts proclaim,
   "Christ is born in Bethlehem!"
Hark, the herald angels sing,
   "Glory to the newborn King!"

Hail the heav'n-born Prince of peace!
   Hail the Sun of Righteousness!
Light and life to all he brings,
   Ris'n with healing in his wings.
Mild he lays his glory by,
   Born that we no more may die,
Born to raise us from the earth,
   Born to give us second birth.
Hark, the herald angels sing,
   "Glory to the newborn King!"

Psalm 98

Sing to the Lord a new song,
the Lord of wonderful deeds.

Shout to the Lord, you earth,
break into song, into praise!

Let the sea roar with its creatures,
the world and all that lives there!
Let rivers clap their hands,
and hills ring out their joy!

The Lord our God comes,
comes to rule the earth,
justly to rule the world,
to govern the peoples aright.

Psalm 98:1a, 4, 7–9

Scripture

See the calendar of readings on the last page of this book. Read the scripture now or at Morning Prayer. After the reading, have a time of silence. The story for the day could be read after this.

Intercessions

At the end of the day we bring our needs before God.

Lord's Prayer.

After the Our Father, we seal our prayer with the greeting of peace.

Scripture Readings for Advent and Christmas

First Sunday of Advent
Mark 13:33–37

Monday	Isaiah 2:2–5
Tuesday	Isaiah 11:1–5
Wednesday	Isaiah 11:6–9
Thursday	Isaiah 25:5–9
Friday	Isaiah 29:17–19
Saturday	Isaiah 30:19–22

Second Sunday of Advent
Matthew 3:1–3

Monday	Isaiah 35:1–6
Tuesday	Isaiah 35:7–10
Wednesday	Isaiah 40:1–5
Thursday	Isaiah 40:6–8
Friday	Isaiah 40:9–11
Saturday	Isaiah 48:17–19

Third Sunday of Advent
John 1:19–23

Monday	Isaiah 45:5–7
Tuesday	Isaiah 54:10
Wednesday	Isaiah 56:1–2
Thursday	Isaiah 61:1–3
Friday	Isaiah 61:9–11
Saturday	Isaiah 42:1–4

Fourth Sunday of Advent
Luke 1:26–38

Weekdays after December 16

December 17	Matthew 1:17
December 18	Matthew 1:18–24
December 19	Luke 1:13–17
December 20	Luke 1:39–45
December 21	Luke 1:46–55
December 22	Luke 1:57–58
December 23	Luke 1:67–75
December 24	Luke 1:76–79

Christmas Day
Luke 2:1–14

The Holy Family
Luke 2:41–52

December 26	Acts 7:54–60
December 27	1 John 1:5
December 28	Matthew 2:13–15
December 29	Luke 2:22
December 30	Luke 2:25–32
December 31	Luke 2:36–38
January 1	Luke 2:16–21
January 2	John 1:25–28
January 3	John 1:29–31
January 4	John 1:35–37
January 5	John 3:11
January 6	Isaiah 60:1–3
January 7	John 5:14

Epiphany of the Lord
Matthew 2:1–11

Weekdays between Epiphany and Baptism of the Lord

Monday	1 John 3:23
Tuesday	1 John 4:7–9
Wednesday	1 John 4:11–12
Thursday	Luke 4:16–19
Friday	Luke 5:12–13
Saturday	John 3:25–30

Baptism of the Lord
Matthew 3:13–17